FOR ORGANS, PIANOS & ELECTRONIC KEYBOARDS

E-Z PLAY TODAY 109

2nd Edition

MOTOWN GREATEST HITS

Contents

ISBN 978-0-7935-1449-6

HAL•LEONARD®
CORPORATION

7777 W. BLUEMOUND RD. P.O. BOX 13819 MILWAUKEE, WI 53213

Visit Hal Leonard Online at
www.halleonard.com

ABC

Registration 9
Rhythm: Rock or 8-Beat

Words and Music by Alphonso Mizell, Frederick Perren,
Deke Richards and Berry Gordy

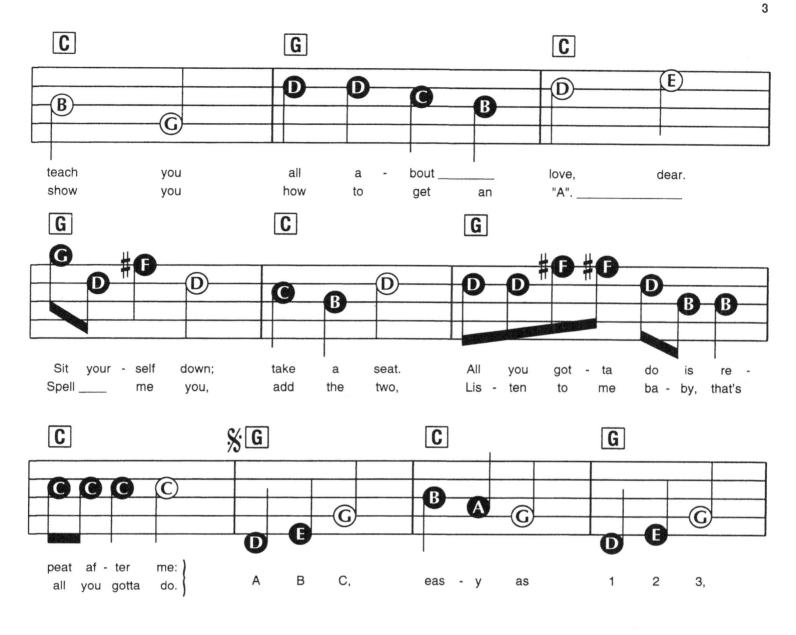

teach you all a - bout _____ love, dear.
show you how to get an "A". _____

Sit your - self down; take a seat. All you got - ta do is re -
Spell ____ me you, add the two, Lis - ten to me ba - by, that's

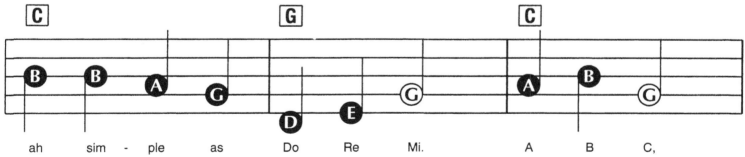

peat af - ter me: ⎫ A B C, eas - y as 1 2 3,
all you gotta do. ⎭

ah sim - ple as Do Re Mi. A B C,

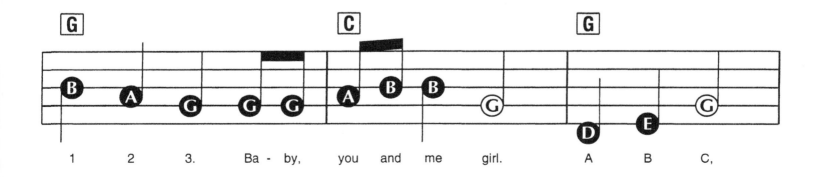

1 2 3. Ba - by, you and me girl. A B C,

4

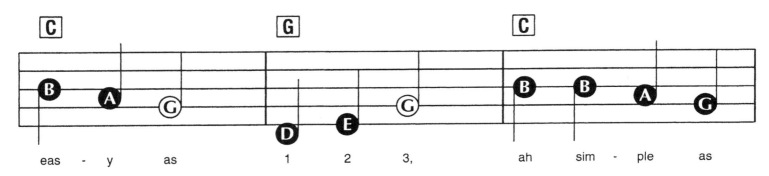

eas - y as 1 2 3, ah sim - ple as

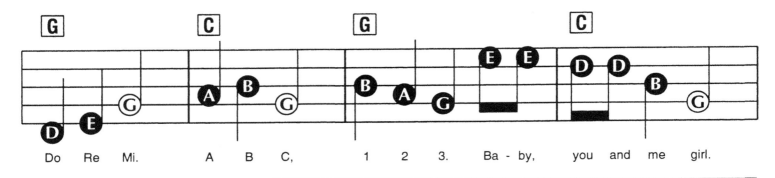

Do Re Mi. A B C, 1 2 3. Ba - by, you and me girl.

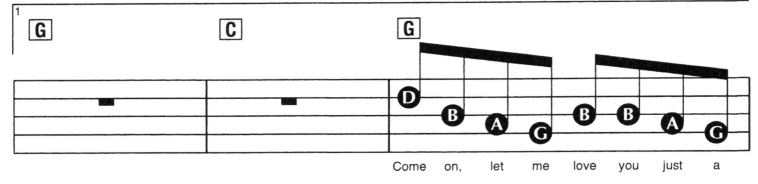

Come on, let me love you just a

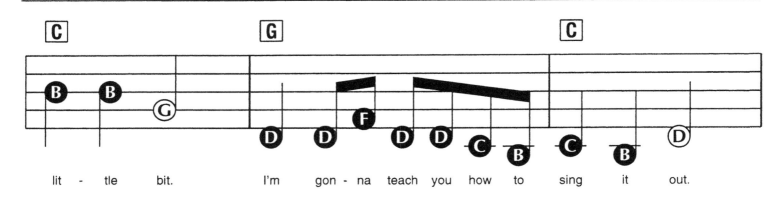

lit - tle bit. I'm gon - na teach you how to sing it out.

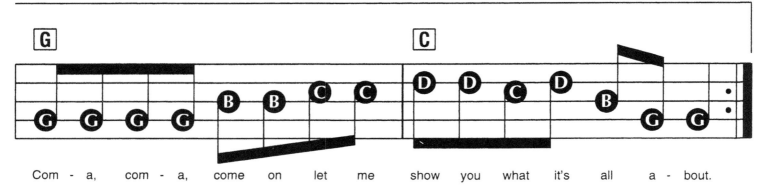

Com - a, com - a, come on let me show you what it's all a - bout.

5

Ain't No Mountain High Enough

Registration 4
Rhythm: Rock or 8-Beat

Words and Music by Nickolas Ashford
and Valerie Simpson

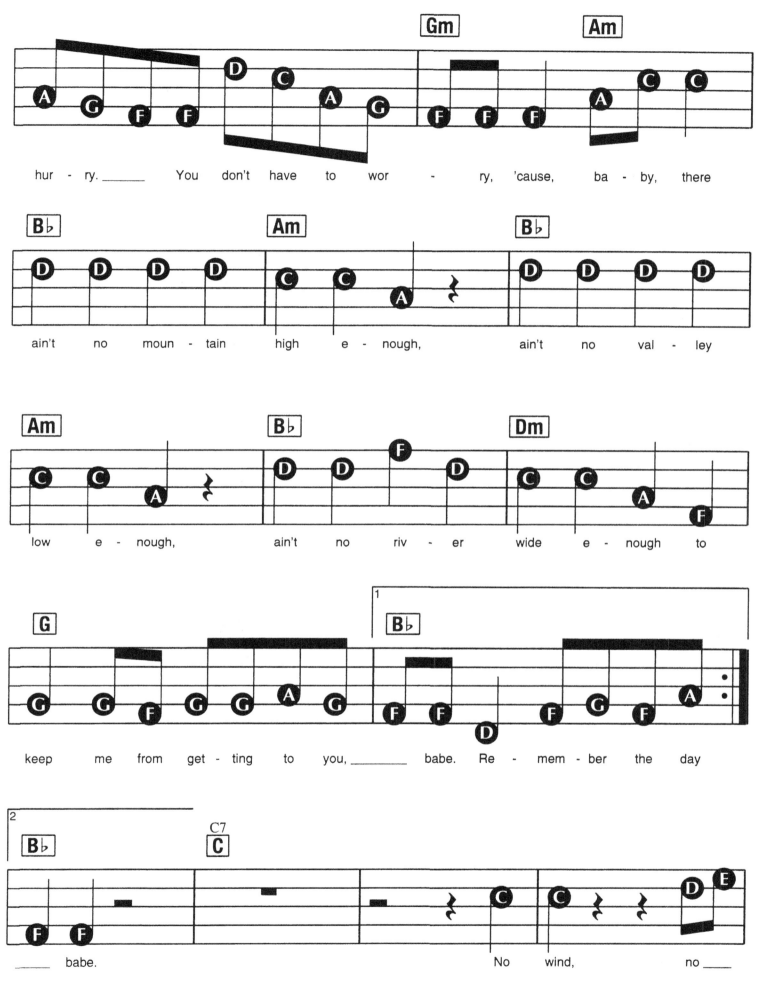

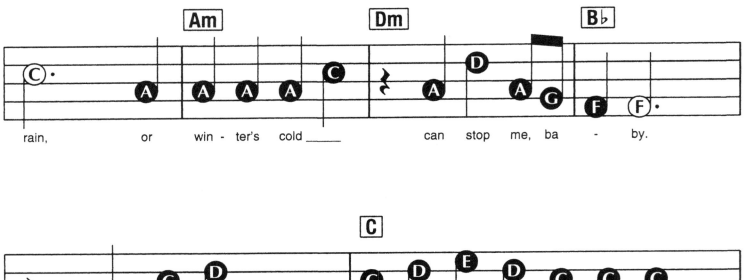

rain,   or   win - ter's   cold _____   can   stop   me, ba - by.

'Cause   you   are   my _____ goal.   If   you're   ev - er   in   trou - ble   I'll   be

D.S. and Fade
(Return to 𝄋
and Fade)

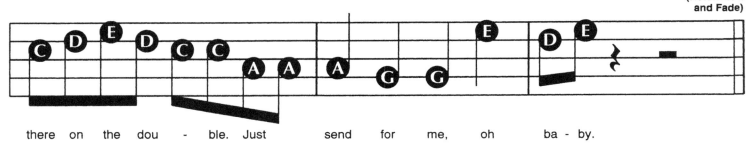

there   on   the   dou - ble.   Just   send   for   me,   oh   ba - by.

Additional Lyrics

2. I set you free.
   I told you you could always count on me.
   From that day on, I made a vow,
   I'll be there when you want me,
   Some way, somehow.
   'Cause baby there *(Chorus)*

3. My love is alive
   Way down in my heart,
   Although we are miles apart.
   If you ever need a helping hand,
   I'll be there on the double
   As fast as I can.
   Don't you know that there *(Chorus)*

Ain't Nothing Like the Real Thing

Registration 4
Rhythm: Rock or 16-Beat

Words and Music by Nickolas Ashford
and Valerie Simpson

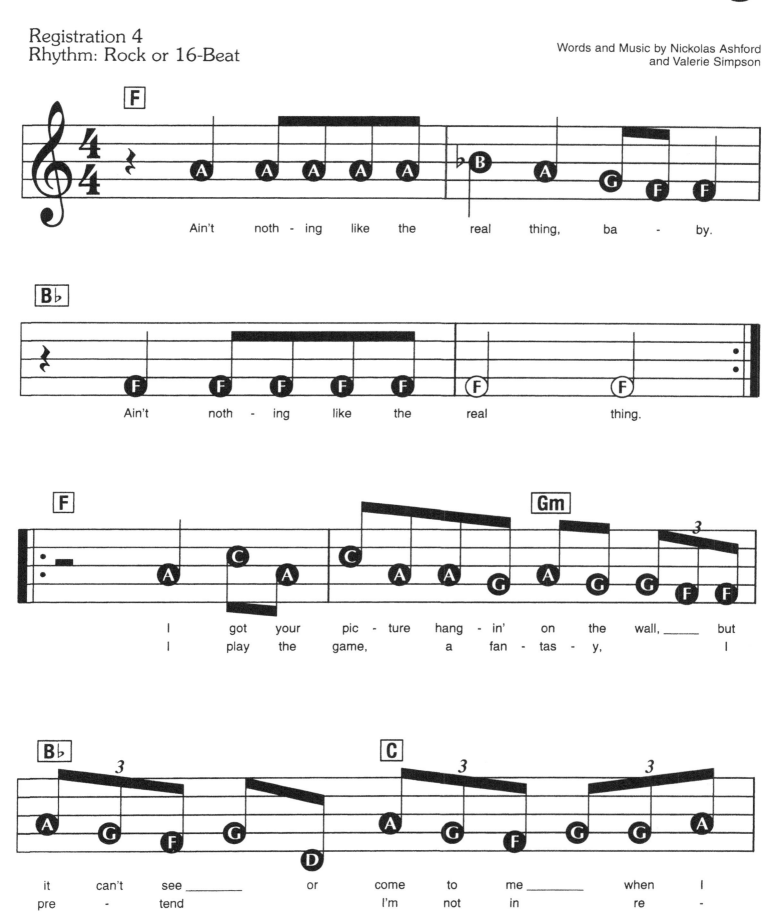

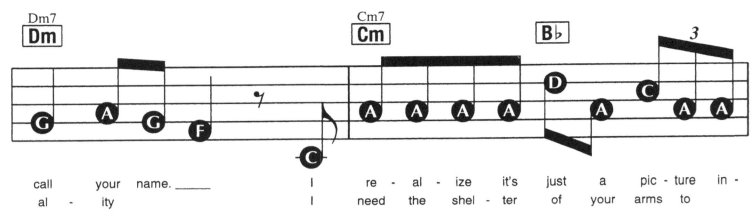

call your name. _____ I re - al - ize it's just a pic - ture in -
al - ity I need the shel - ter of your arms to

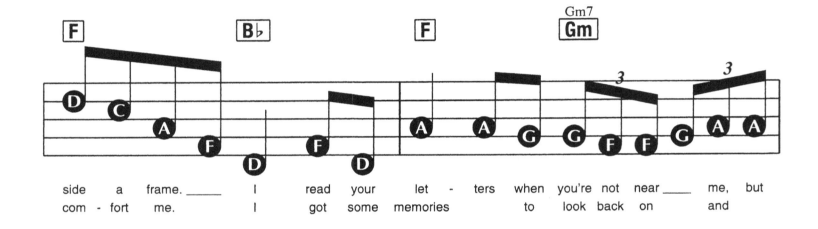

side a frame. _____ I read your let - ters when you're not near _____ me, but
com - fort me. I got some memories to look back on and

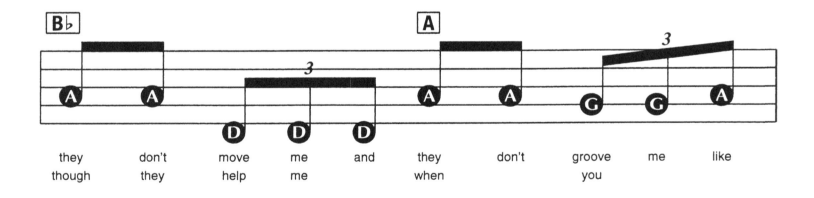

they don't move me and they don't groove me like
though they help me when you

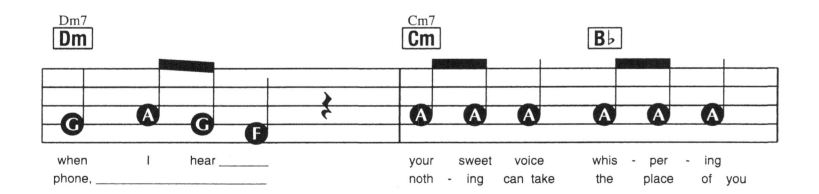

when I hear _____ your sweet voice whis - per - ing
phone, _____ noth - ing can take the place of you

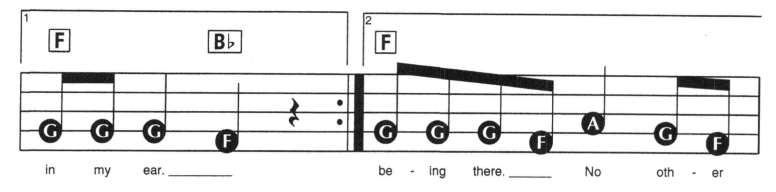

in my ear. _____   be - ing there. _____ No oth - er

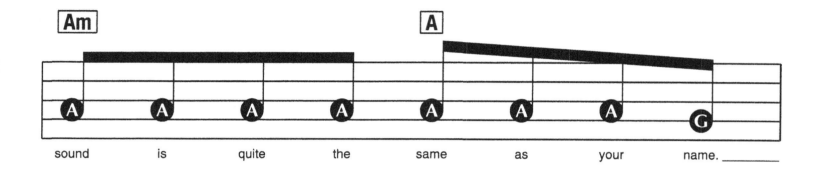

sound   is   quite   the   same   as   your   name. _____

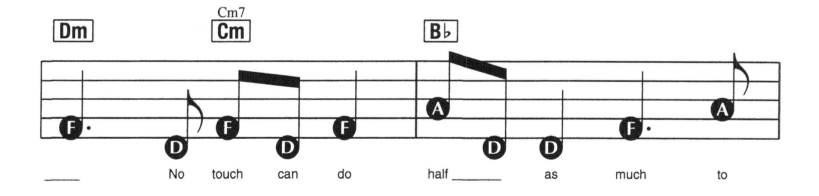

_____   No touch can do half _____ as much to

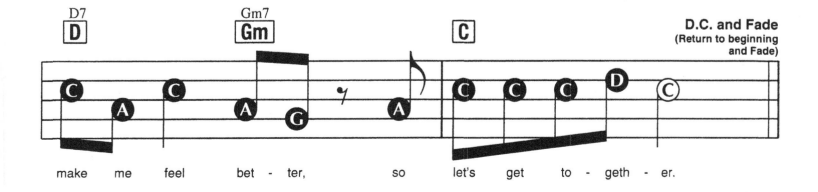

make me feel bet - ter,   so   let's get to - geth - er.

D.C. and Fade
(Return to beginning
and Fade)

12

Ain't Too Proud to Beg

Registration 4
Rhythm: Rock or 8-Beat

Words and Music by Edward Holland
and Norman Whitfield

1. I know you wan - na leave me, but I re - fuse to let you
2.-4. *See additional lyrics*

go. If I have to beg, plead for your sym - pa - thy, I don't

mind 'cause you mean that much to me. Ain't too proud to beg and you

know it. Please don't leave me, girl, don't you go. Ain't too proud to

© 1966 (Renewed 1994) JOBETE MUSIC CO., INC.
All Rights Controlled and Administered by EMI BLACKWOOD MUSIC INC. on behalf of STONE AGATE MUSIC (A Division of JOBETE MUSIC CO., INC.)
All Rights Reserved   International Copyright Secured   Used by Permission

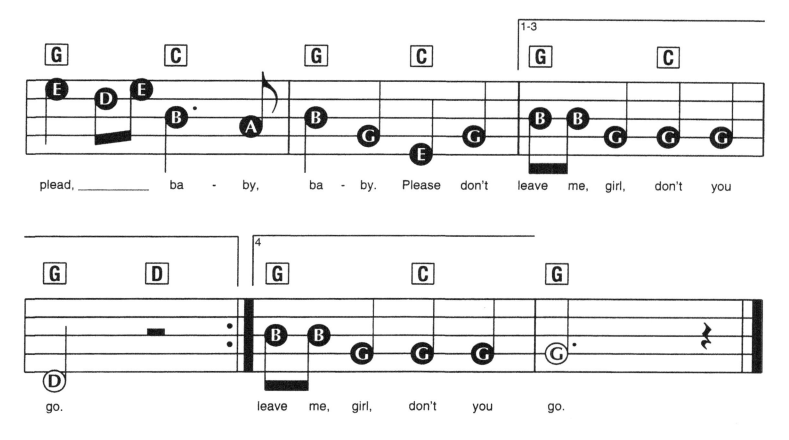

plead, _____ ba - by, ba - by. Please don't leave me, girl, don't you

go.　　　　leave me, girl, don't you go.

Additional Lyrics

2. Now, I've heard a cryin' man
   Is half a man with no sense of pride.
   But if I have to cry to keep you,
   I don't mind weepin' if it'll keep you by my side.

3. If I have to sleep on your doorstep all night and day
   Just to keep you from walking away,
   Let your friends laugh, even this I can stand,
   'Cause I wanna keep you any way I can.

4. Now I've got a love so deep in the pit of my heart
   and each day it grows more and more.
   I'm not ashamed to call and plead to you, baby,
   If pleading keeps you from walking out that door.

Baby Love

Registration 3
Rhythm: Swing or Shuffle

Words and Music by Brian Holland,
Edward Holland and Lamont Dozier

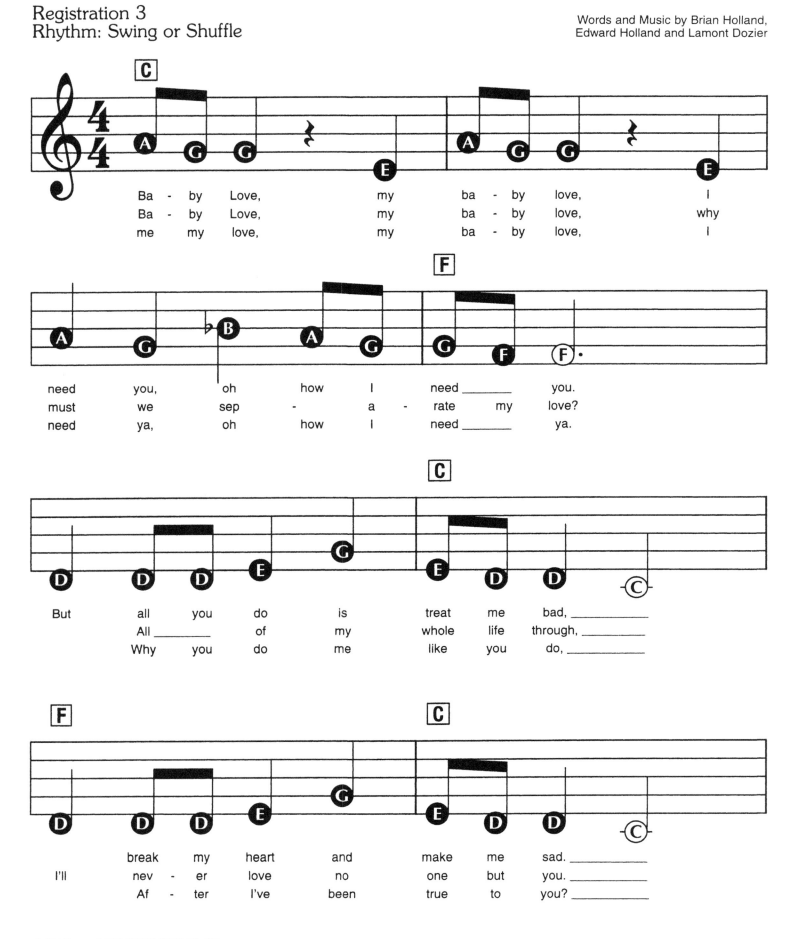

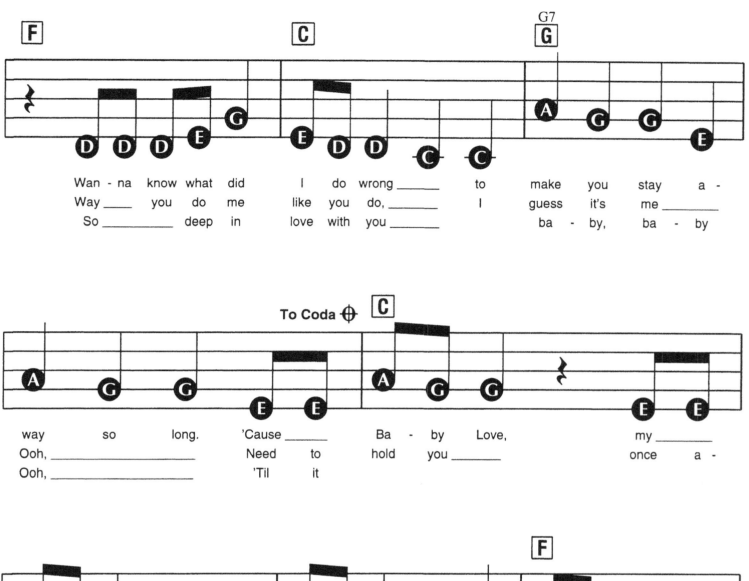

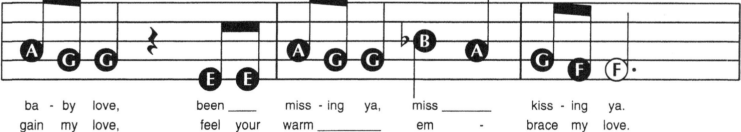

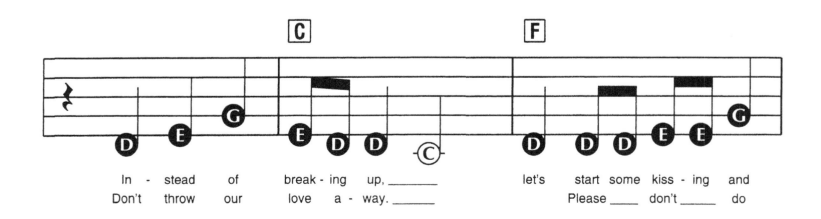

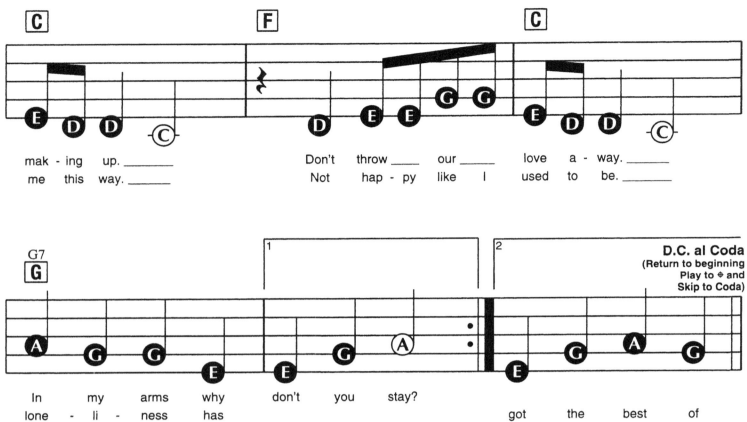

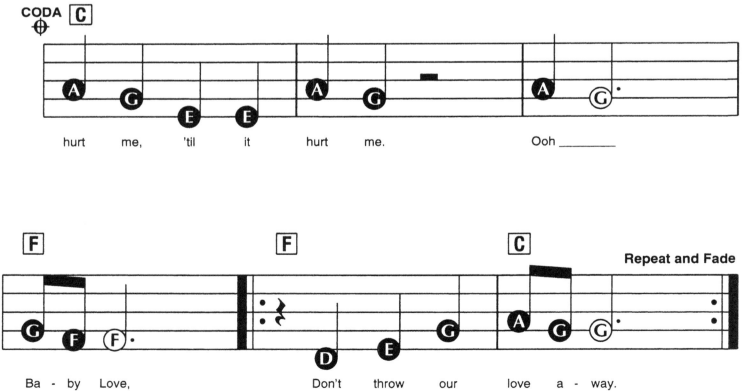

Ben

Registration 1
Rhythm: Pops or 8 Beat

Words by Don Black
Music by Walter Scharf

18

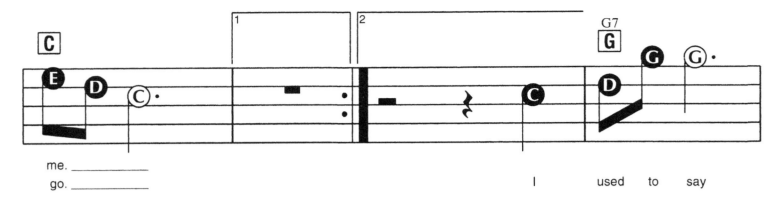

me. _____
go. _____   I   used   to   say

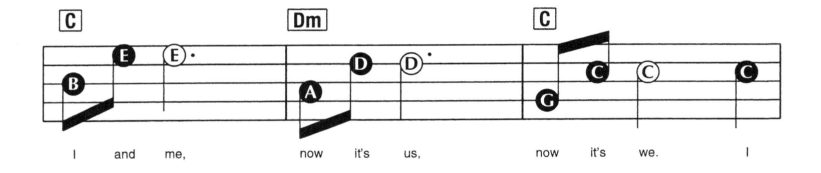

I   and   me,   now   it's   us,   now   it's   we.   I

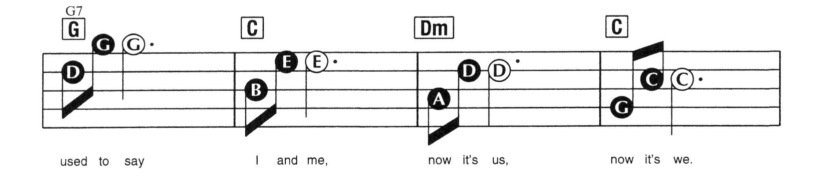

used   to   say   I   and   me,   now   it's   us,   now   it's   we.

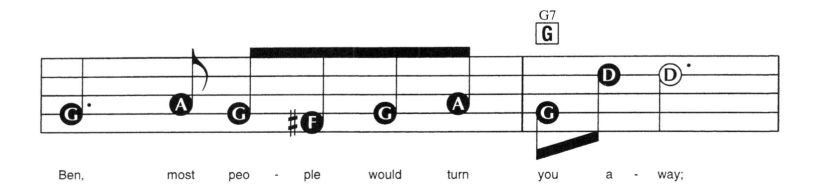

Ben,   most   peo - ple   would   turn   you   a - way;

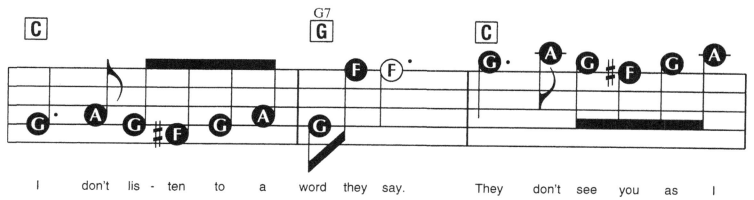

I don't lis-ten to a word they say. They don't see you as I

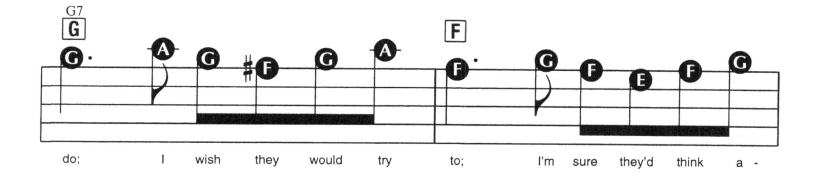

do; I wish they would try to; I'm sure they'd think a-

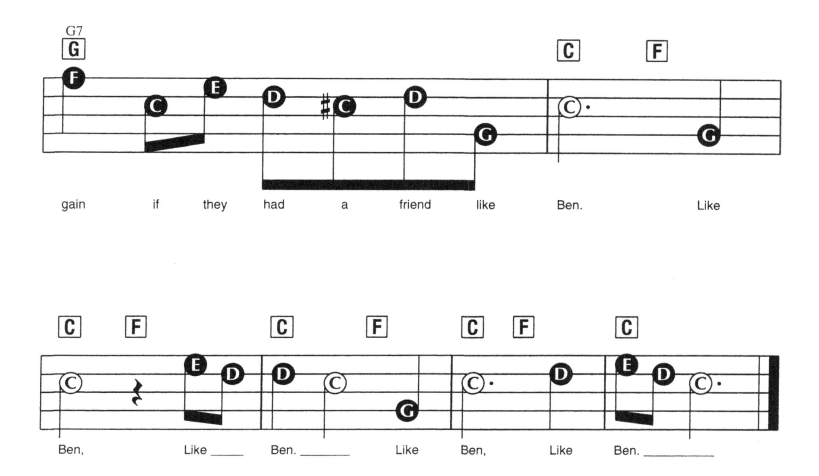

gain if they had a friend like Ben. Like

Ben, Like _____ Ben. _____ Like Ben, Like _____ Ben. _____

Bernadette

Registration 2
Rhythm: 8 Beat or Rock

Words and Music by Brian Holland,
Lamont Dozier and Edward Holland

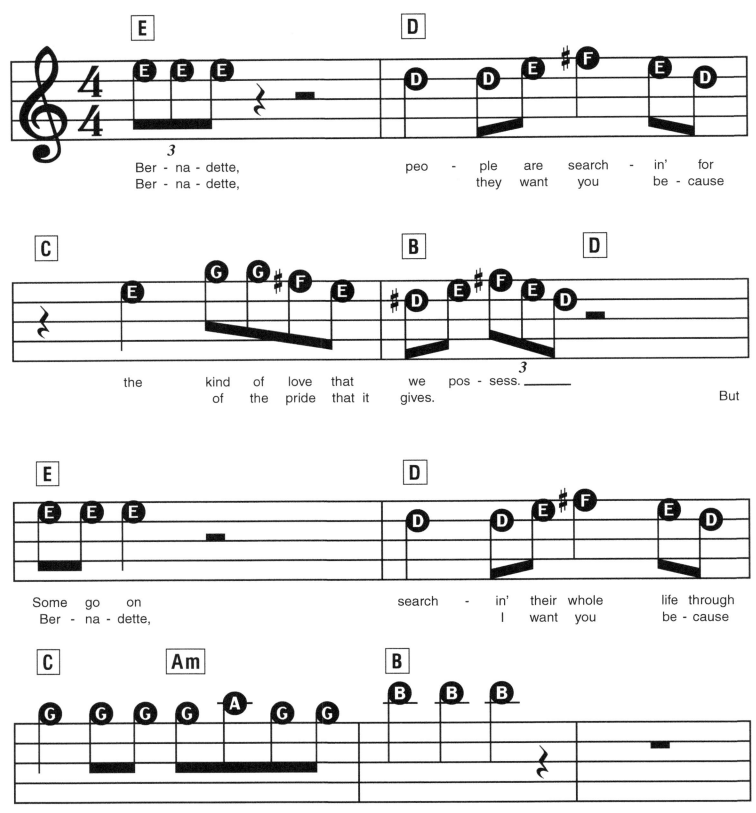

21

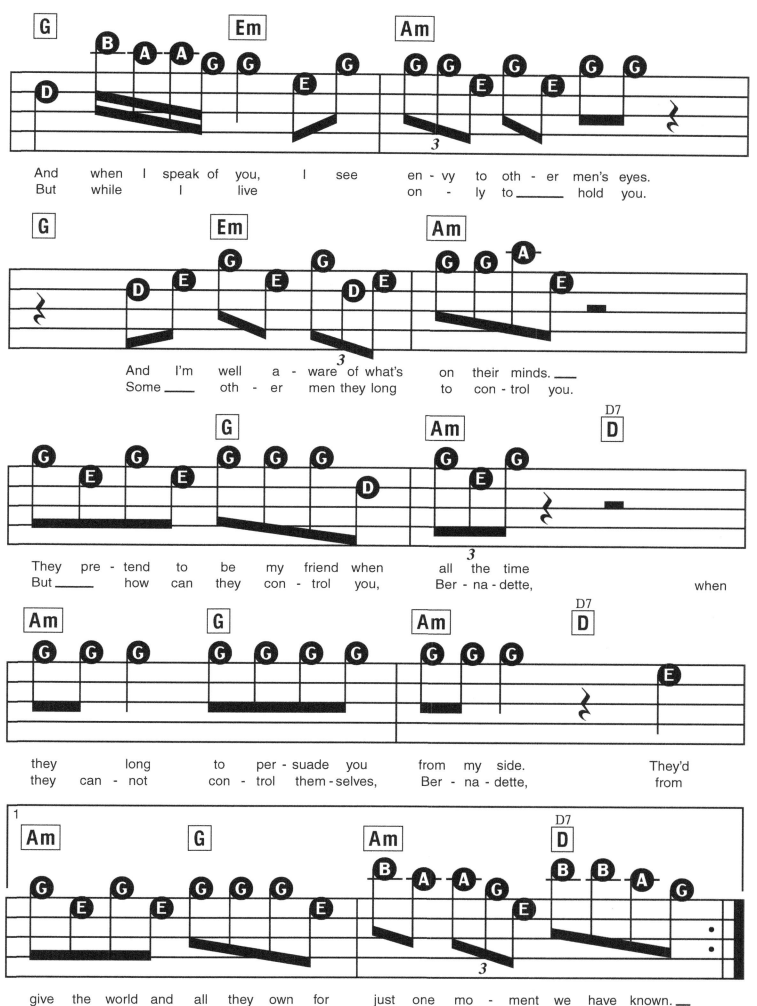

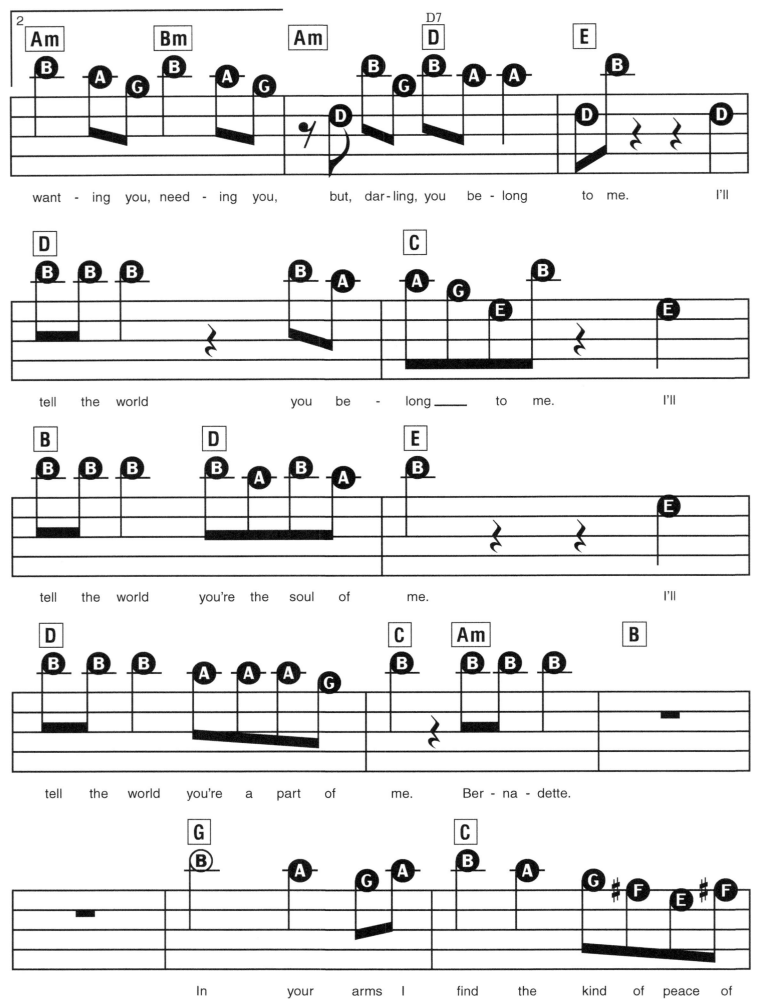

23

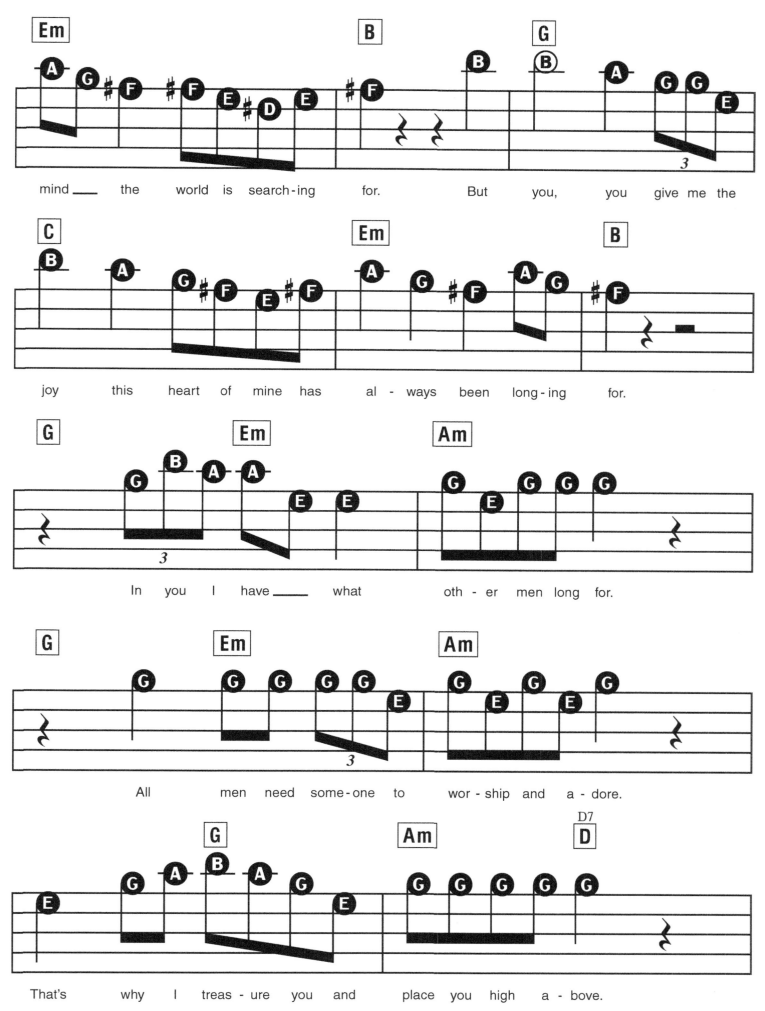

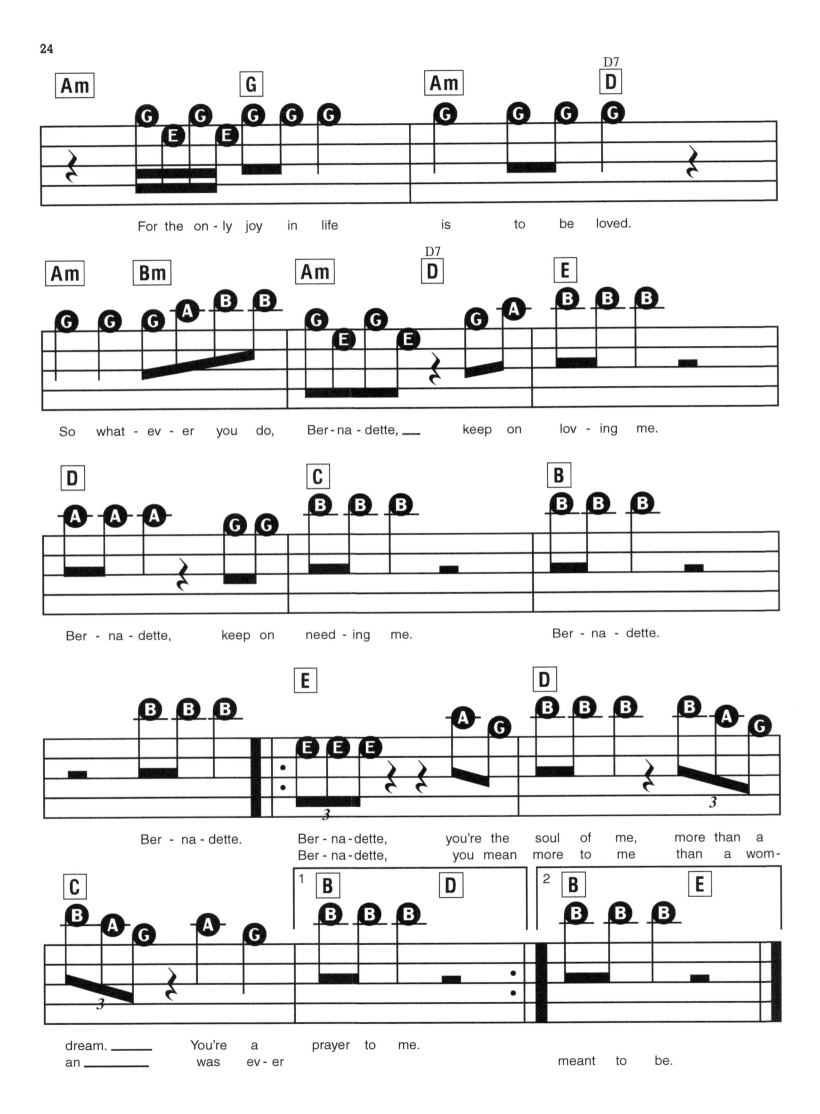

For the on-ly joy in life   is   to   be loved.

So what - ev - er you do,   Ber - na - dette, ___ keep on lov - ing me.

Ber - na - dette,   keep on   need - ing me.   Ber - na - dette.

Ber - na - dette.   Ber - na - dette,   you're the   soul of me,   more than a
                     Ber - na - dette,   you mean   more to me   than a wom-

dream. ___ You're a   prayer to me.
an ___ was ev - er   meant to be.

Dancing in the Street

Registration 5
Rhythm: Rock or 8 Beat

Words and Music by Marvin Gaye,
Ivy Hunter and William Stevenson

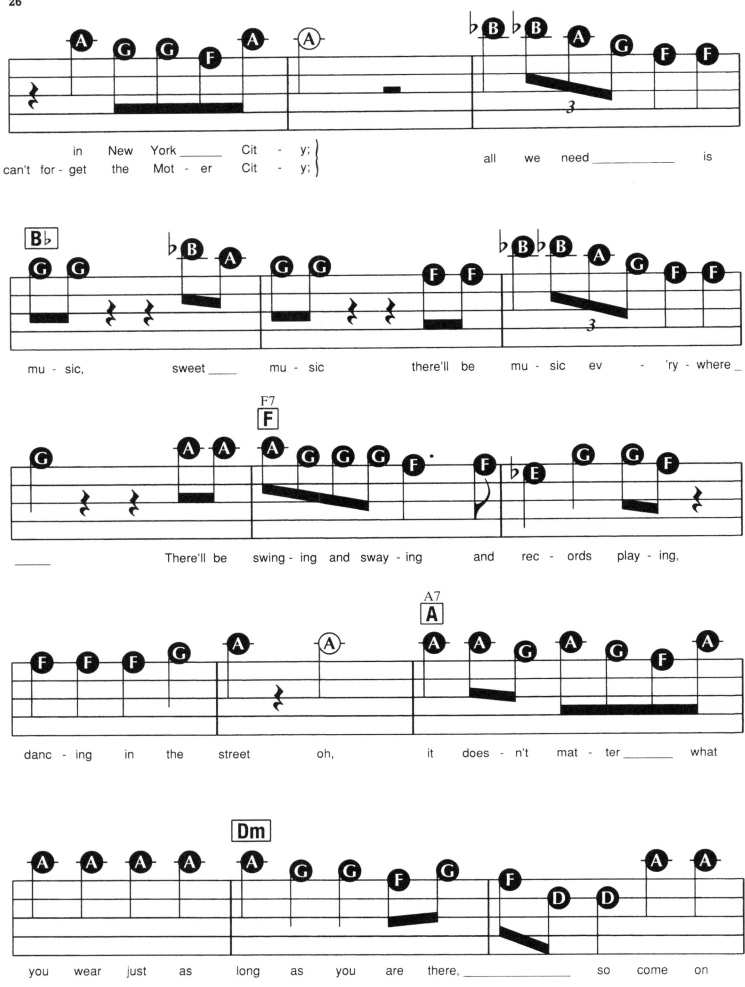

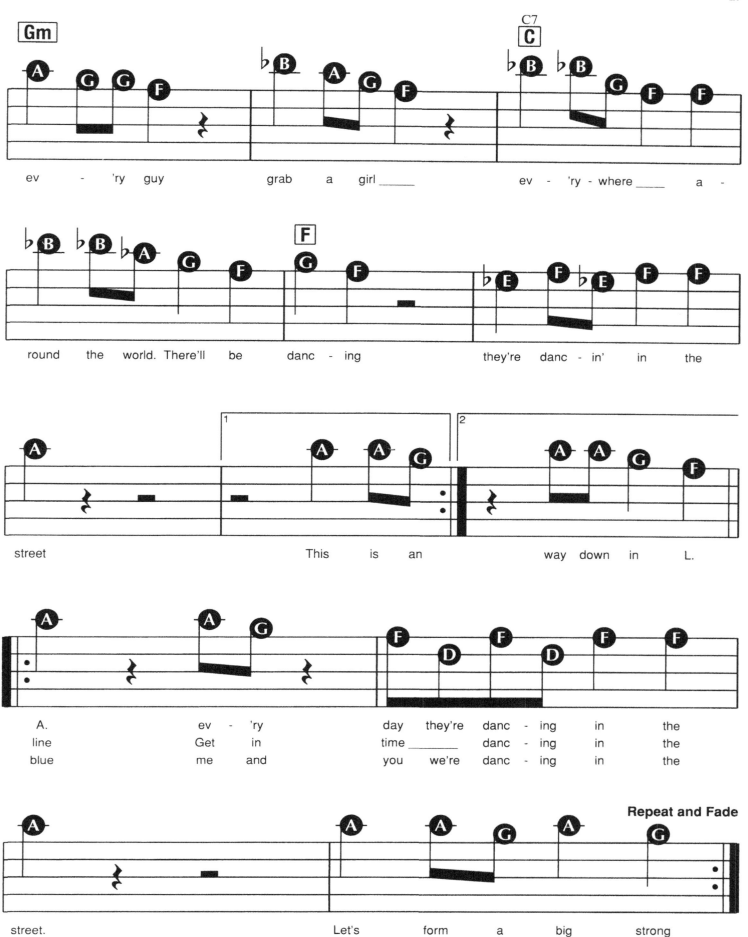

ev - 'ry guy   grab a girl _____   ev - 'ry - where _____ a -

round the world. There'll be danc - ing   they're danc - in' in the

street   This is an   way down in L.

A.   ev - 'ry   day they're danc - ing in the
line   Get   in   time _____ danc - ing in the
blue   me and   you we're danc - ing in the

Repeat and Fade

street.   Let's   form   a   big   strong
street.   A -   cross   the   o -   cean
street.   Way   down   in   L.

Do You Love Me

Registration 7
Rhythm: Rock or 8-Beat

Words and Music by
Berry Gordy

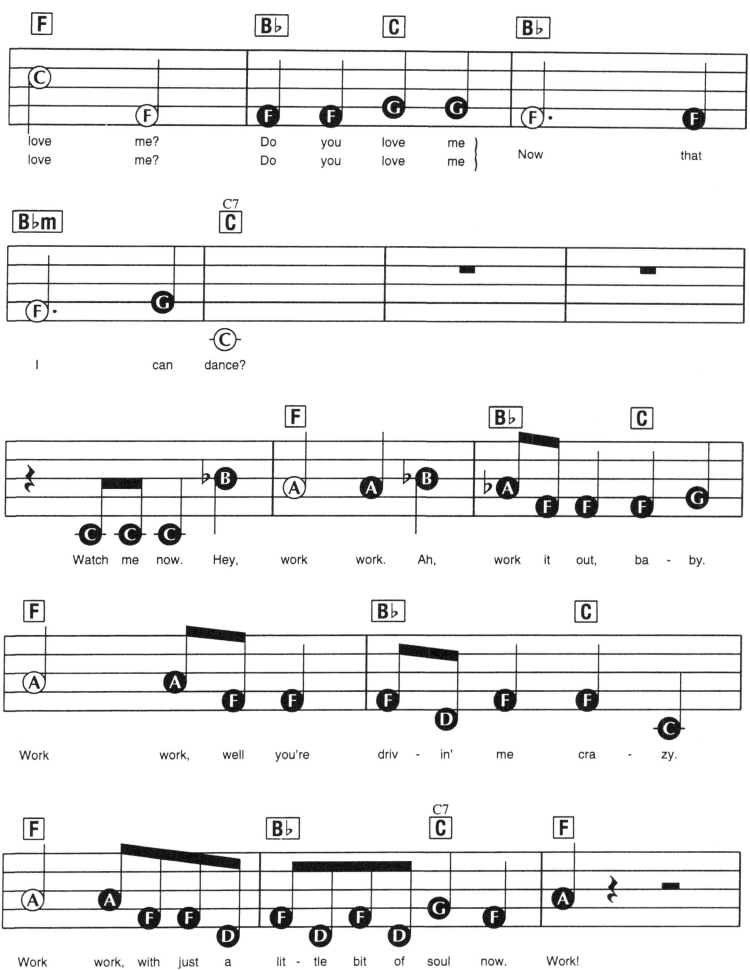

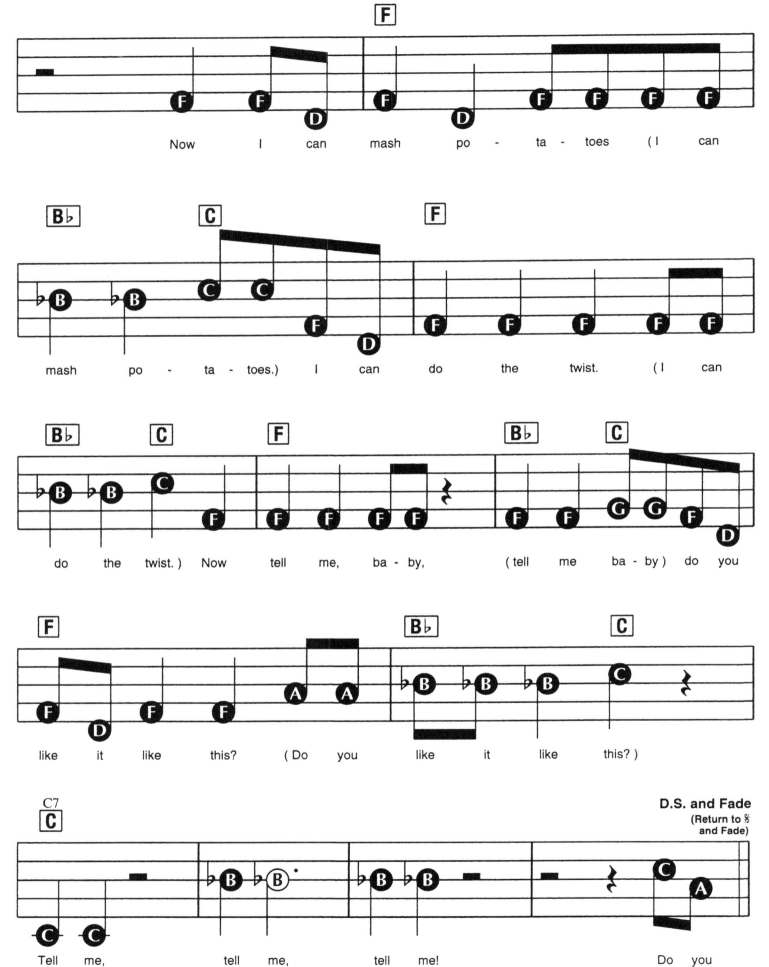

How Sweet It Is
(To Be Loved by You)

Registration 5
Rhythm: Shuffle or Swing

Words and Music by Edward Holland,
Lamont Dozier and Brian Holland

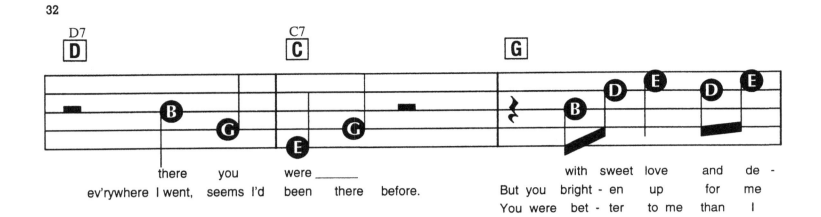

there you were _____
ev'rywhere I went, seems I'd been there before.

with sweet love and de -
But you bright - en up for me
You were bet - ter to me than I

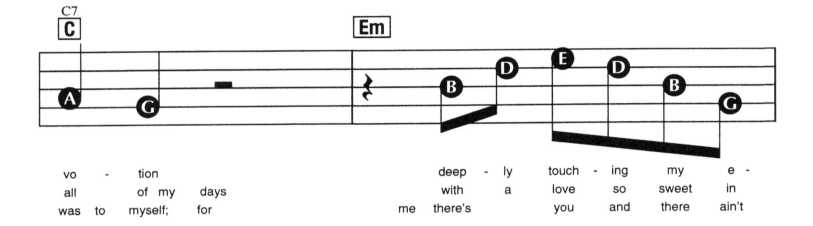

vo - tion
all of my days
was to myself; for

deep - ly touch - ing my e -
with a love so sweet in
me there's you and there ain't

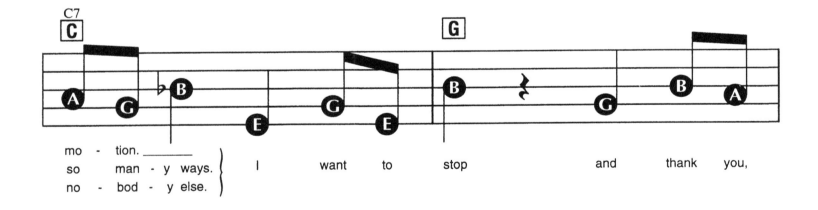

mo - tion. _____
so man - y ways.
no - bod - y else.

I want to stop and thank you,

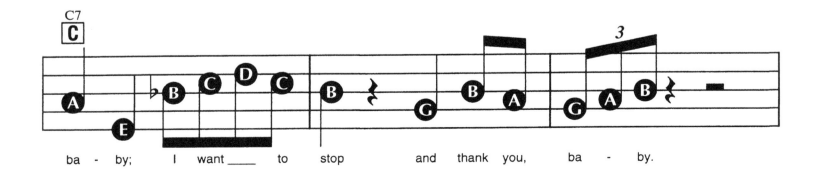

ba - by; I want ____ to stop and thank you, ba - by.

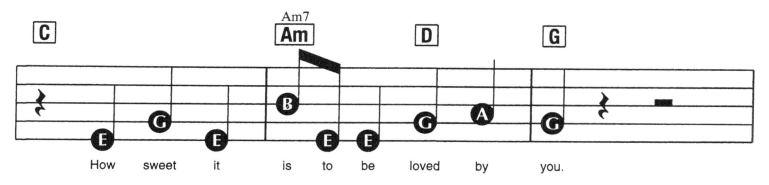

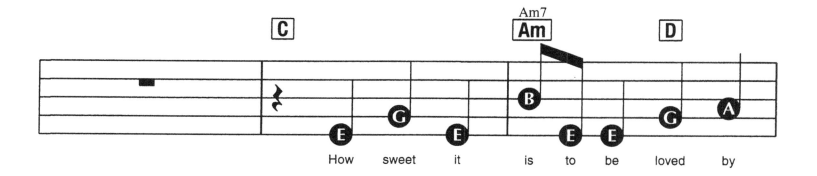

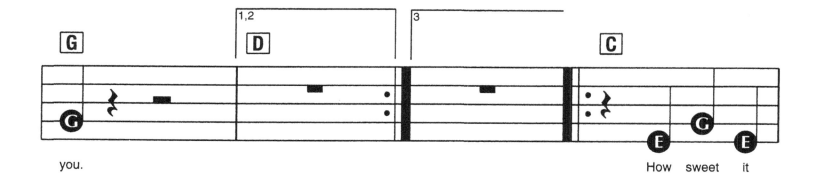

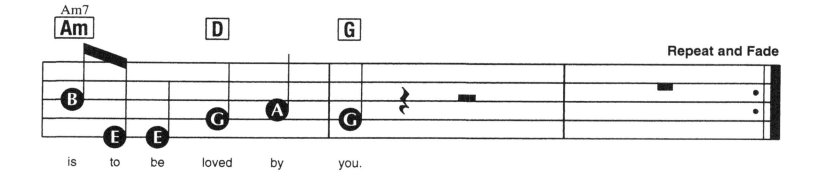

Easy

Registration 3
Rhythm: Pops or 8 Beat

Words and Music by
Lionel Richie

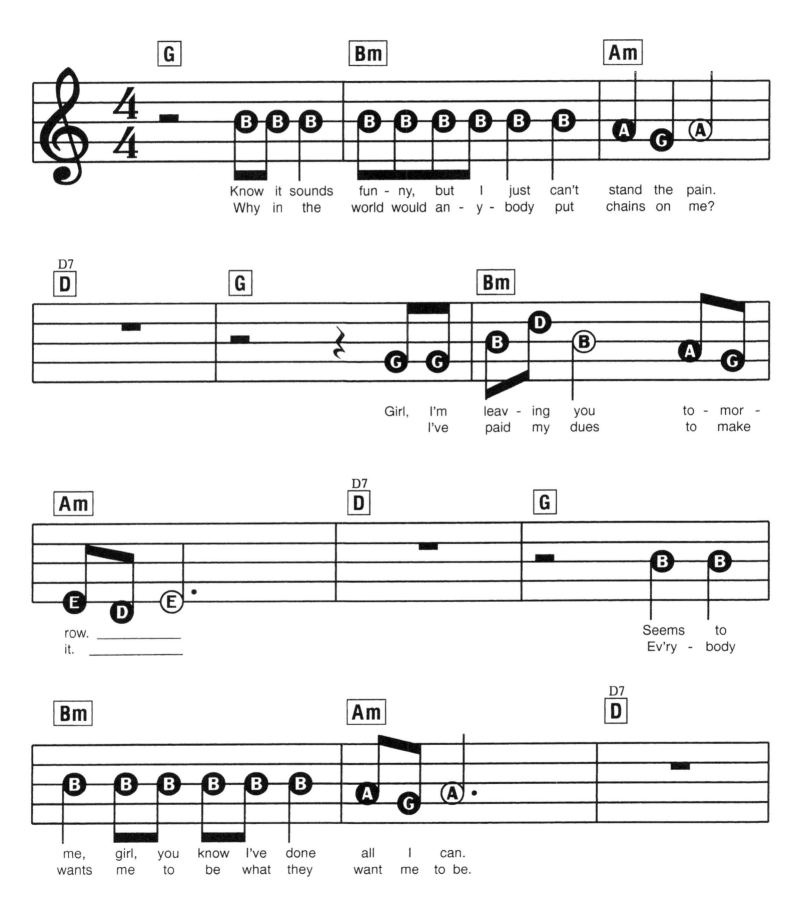

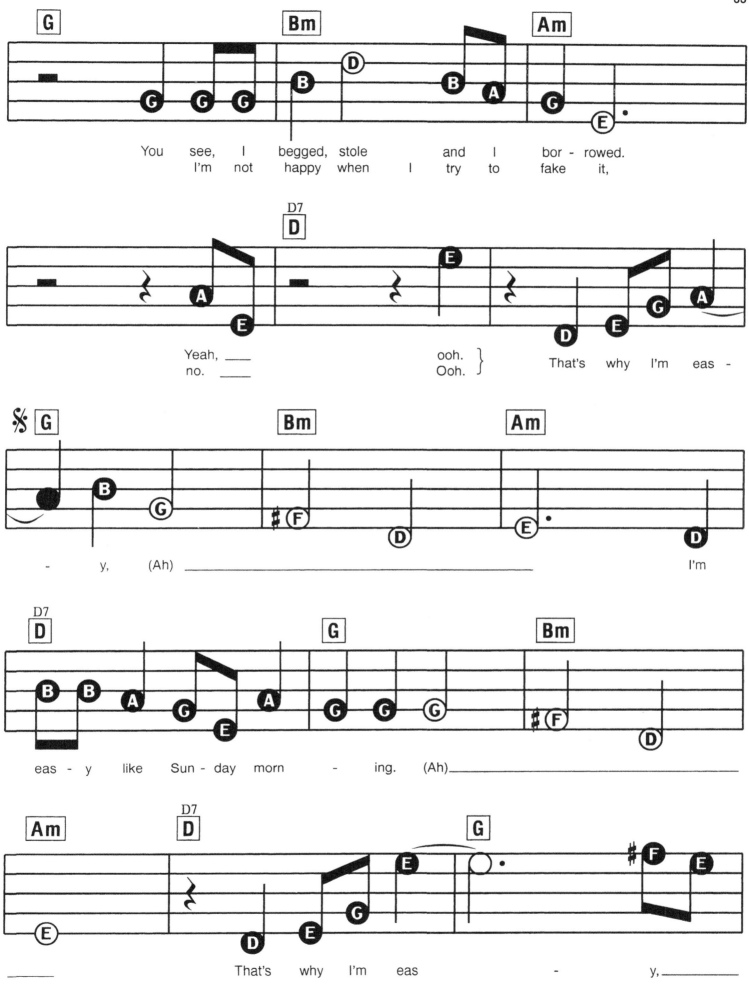

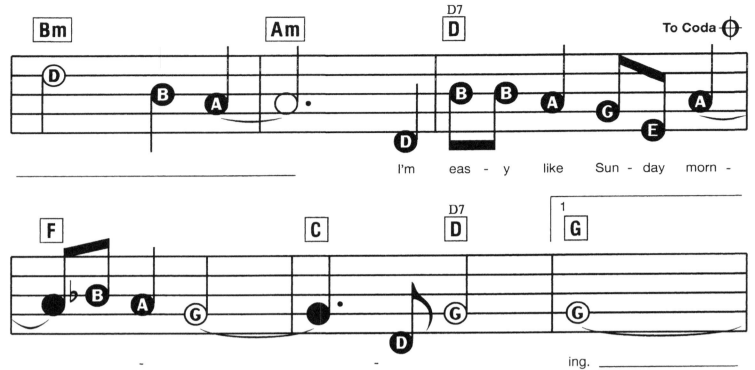

I'm eas - y like Sun - day morn -

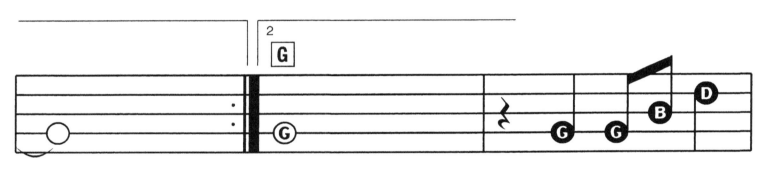

- - ing. _____

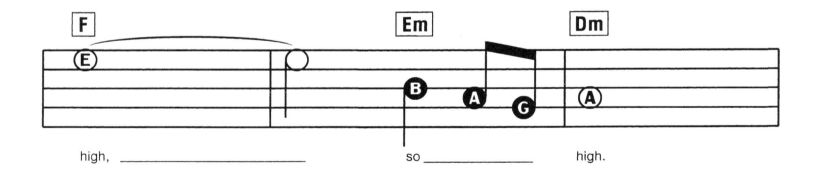

_____ ing. I wan - na be

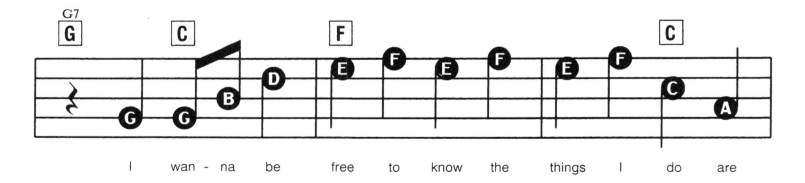

high, _____ so _____ high.

G - C - F - C

I wan - na be free to know the things I do are

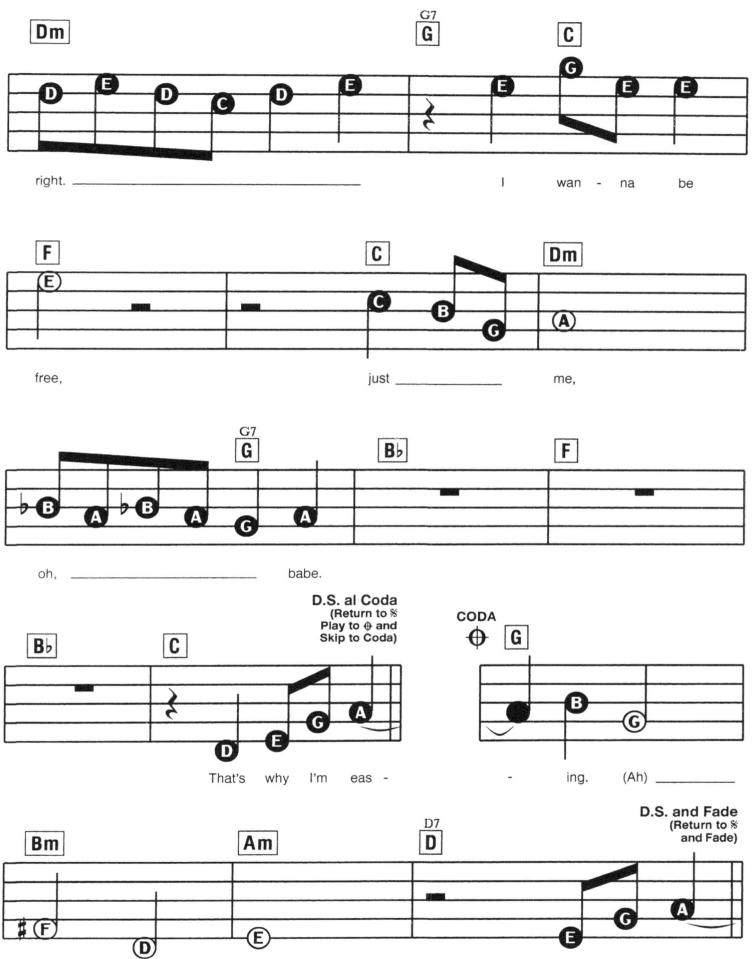

For Once in My Life

Registration 8
Rhythm: Rock or Pops

Words by Ronald Miller
Music by Orlando Murden

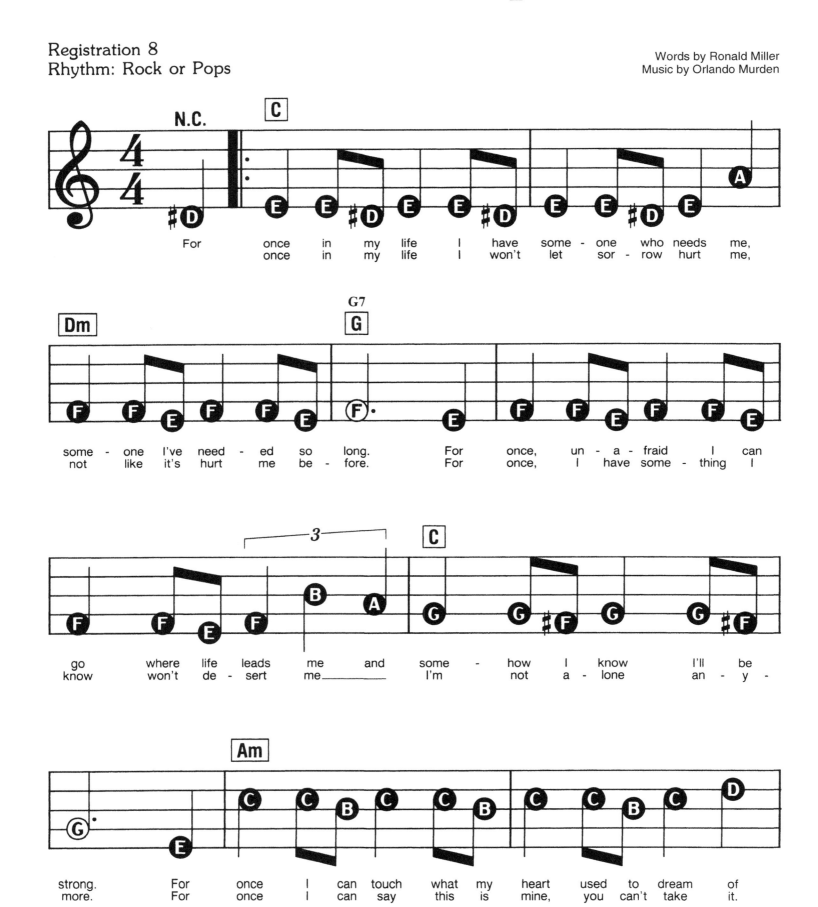

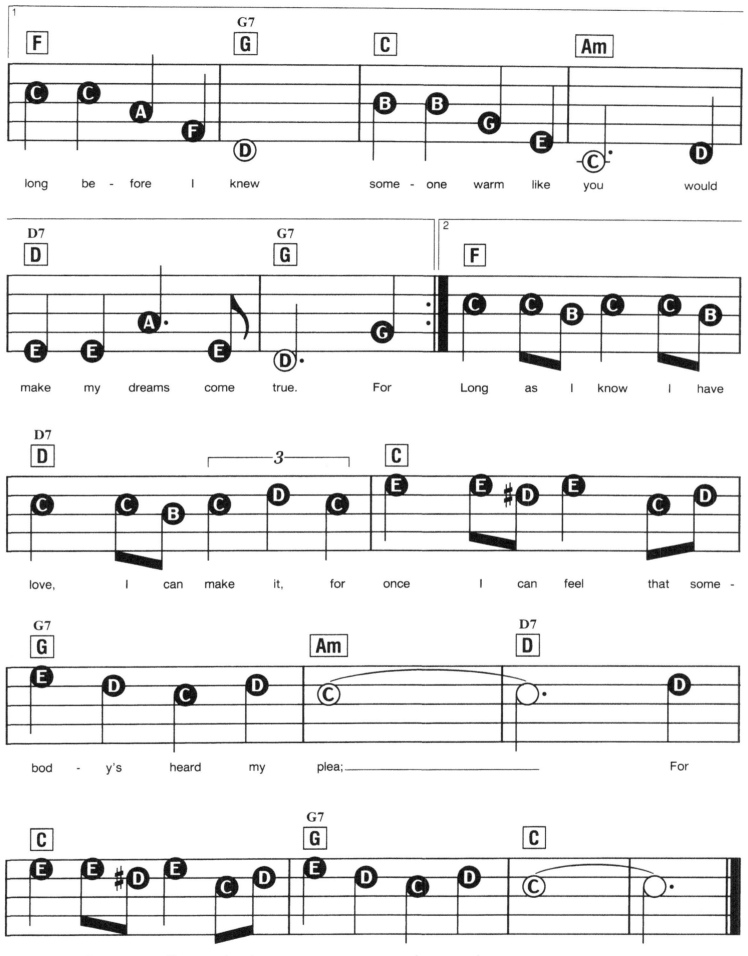

Get Ready

Registration 8
Rhythm: R&B or 8 Beat

Words and Music by
William "Smokey" Robinson

41

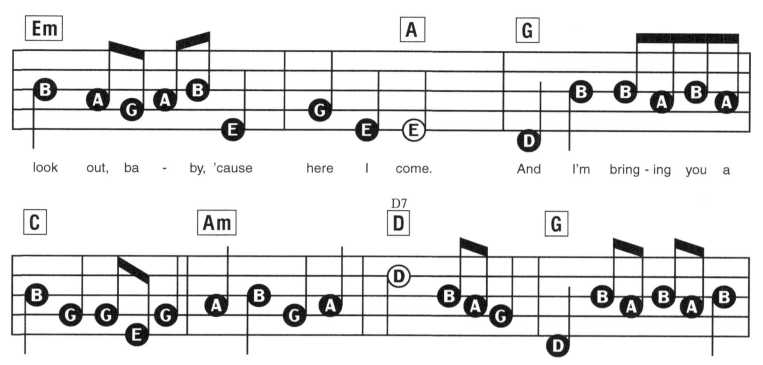

look out, ba - by, 'cause here I come. And I'm bring-ing you a

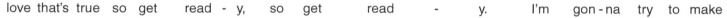

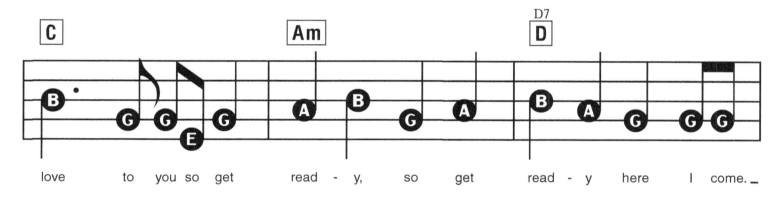

love that's true so get read - y, so get read - y. I'm gon-na try to make

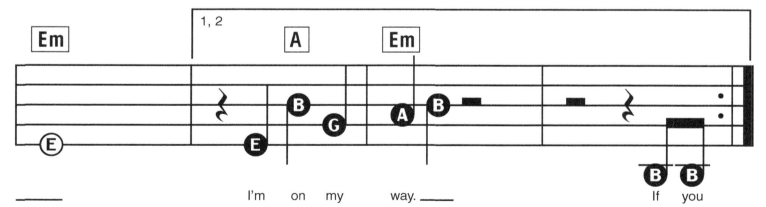

love to you so get read - y, so get read - y here I come.

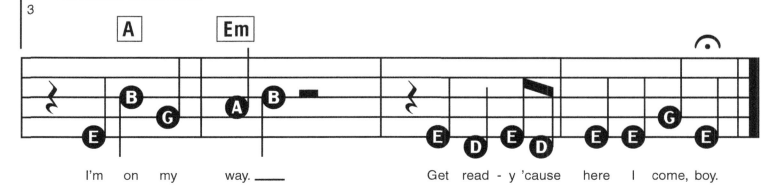

I'm on my way.   If you

I'm on my way.   Get read - y 'cause here I come, boy.

Heatwave
(Love Is Like a Heatwave)

Registration 4
Rhythm: Swing or Shuffle

Words and Music by Edward Holland,
Lamont Dozier and Brian Holland

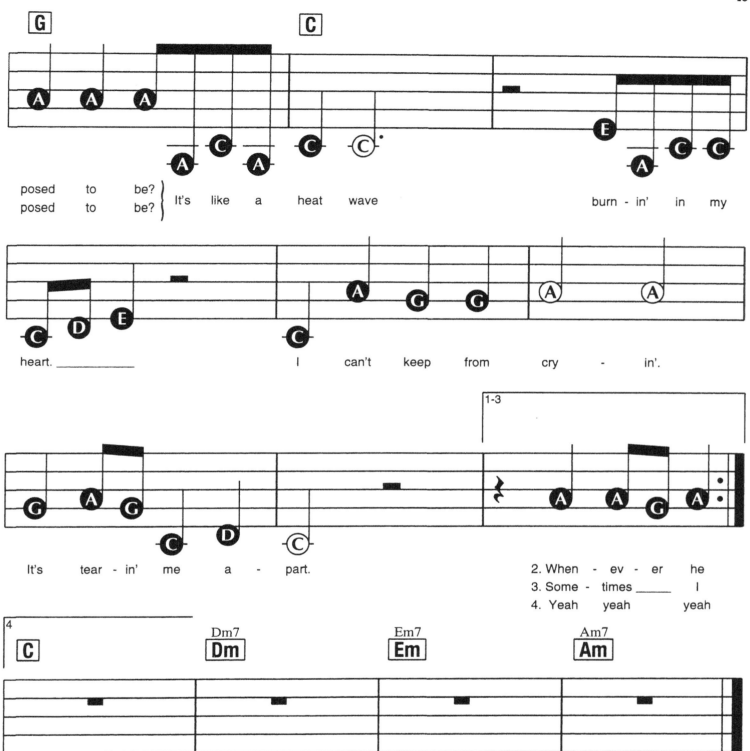

G   C

posed   to   be?
posed   to   be?   It's like a heat wave   burn - in' in my

heart. _____   I can't keep from cry - in'.

1-3

It's tear - in' me a - part.   2. When - ev - er he
                                            3. Some - times _____ I
                                            4. Yeah yeah yeah

4
C   Dm7   Em7   Am7
                  Dm   Em   Am

Additional Lyrics

3. Sometimes I stare into space,
   tears all over my face.
   I can't explain it,
   Don't understand it.
   I ain't never felt like this before.
   Now that funny feelin' has me amazed.
   I don't know what to do, my head's in a haze.

4. Yeah yeah yeah yeah yeah
   yeah whoa ho.
   Yeah yeah yeah yeah ho.
   Don't pass up this chance.
   This time it's a true romance.

I Can't Get Next to You

Registration 2
Rhythm: Rock or Funk

Words and Music by Barrett Strong
and Norman Whitfield

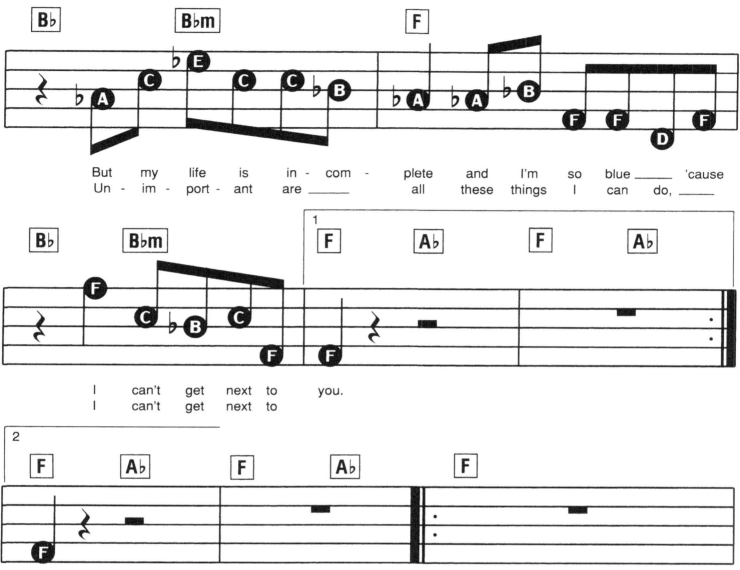

But my life is in - com - plete and I'm so blue _____ 'cause
Un - im - port - ant are _____ all these things I can do, _____

I can't get next to you.
I can't get next to

you.

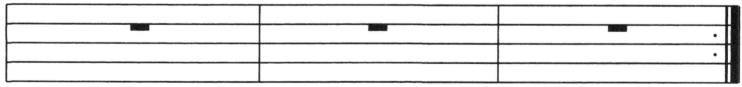

(Spoken:) I can turn back the hands of time, you
I can change anything from old

better believe I can. I can make the seasons change just by waving my hand.
to new. The things I want to do the most I'm unable to do.

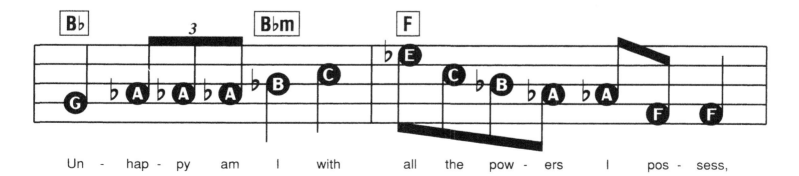

Un - hap - py am I with all the pow - ers I pos - sess,

'cause girl, _____ you're the key to my hap-pi-ness. And

I, _____ I, _____ I _____

can't get next to you, girl, you're blow-in' my mind.

I can't get next to you. Can't you see these tears I'm

Repeat and Fade

cry-in'? I can't get next to you. Girl, _____ it's you that I need.

I Second That Emotion

Registration 9
Rhythm: Rock or 16-Beat

Words and Music by William "Smokey" Robinson
and Alfred Cleveland

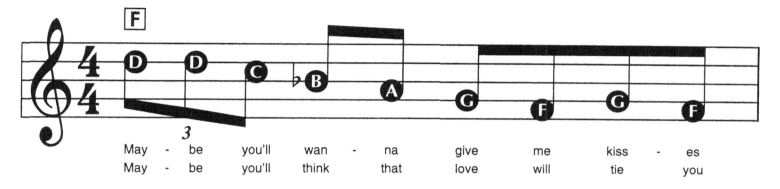

May - be you'll wan - na give me kiss - es
May - be you'll think that love will tie you

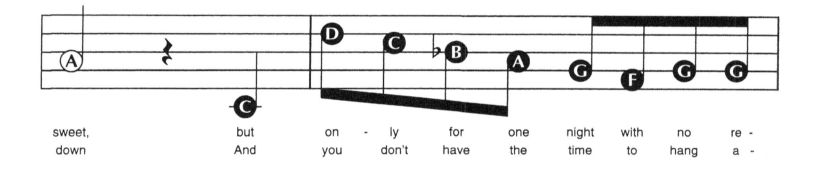

sweet, but on - ly for one night with no re -
down And you don't have the time to hang a -

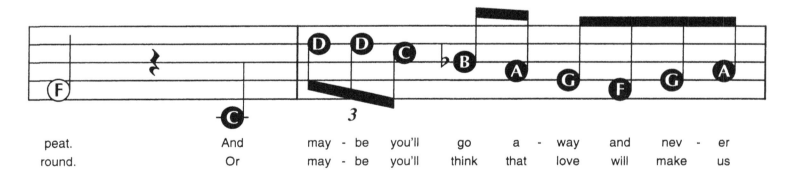

peat. And may - be you'll go a - way and nev - er
round. Or may - be you'll think that love will make us

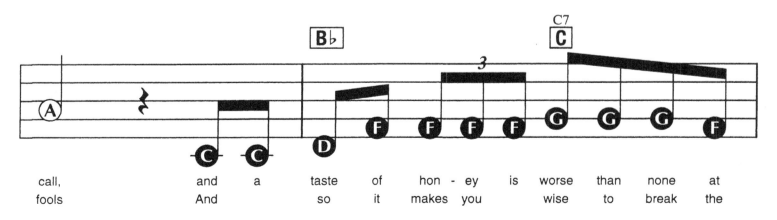

call, and a taste of hon - ey is worse than none at
fools And so it makes you wise to break the

48

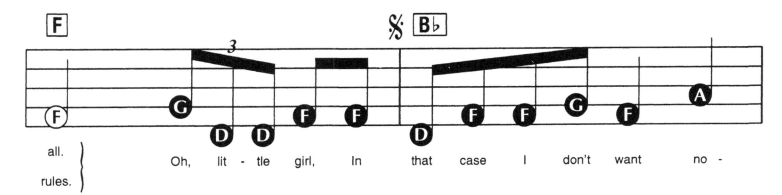

all.
rules.

Oh, lit - tle girl, In that case I don't want no -

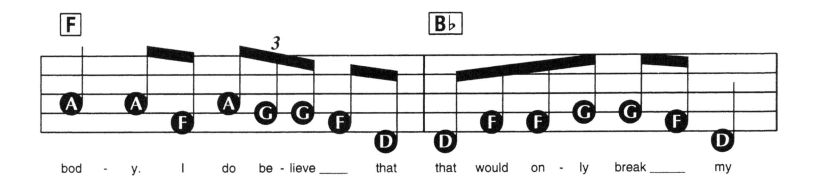

bod - y. I do be - lieve ____ that that would on - ly break ____ my

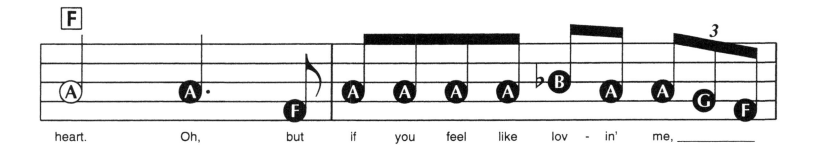

heart. Oh, but if you feel like lov - in' me, _____

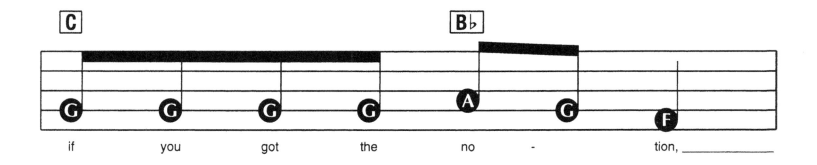

if you got the no - tion, _____

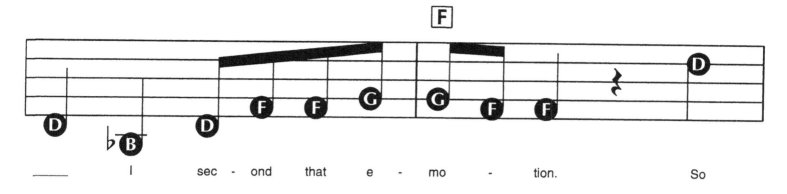

_____ I sec - ond that e - mo - tion. So

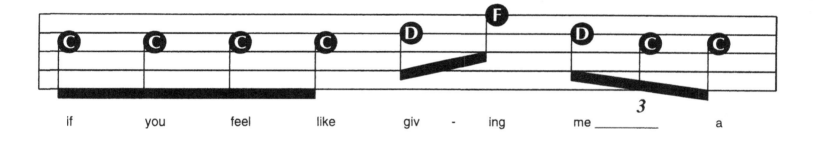

if you feel like giv - ing me _____ a

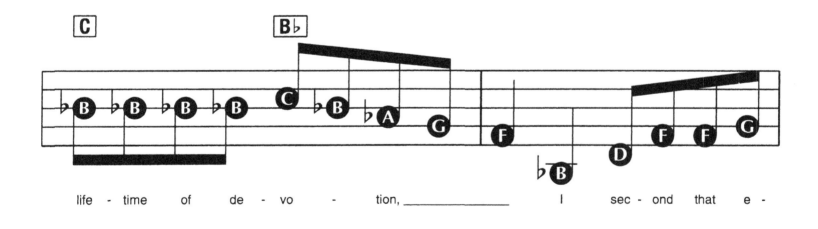

life - time of de - vo - tion, _____ I sec - ond that e -

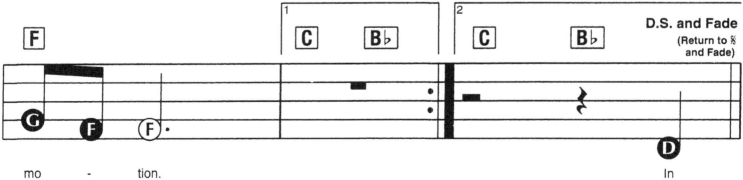

mo - tion. In

I Can't Help Myself
(Sugar Pie, Honey Bunch)

Registration 9
Rhythm: Rock or 8-Beat

Words and Music by Brian Holland,
Lamont Dozier and Edward Holland

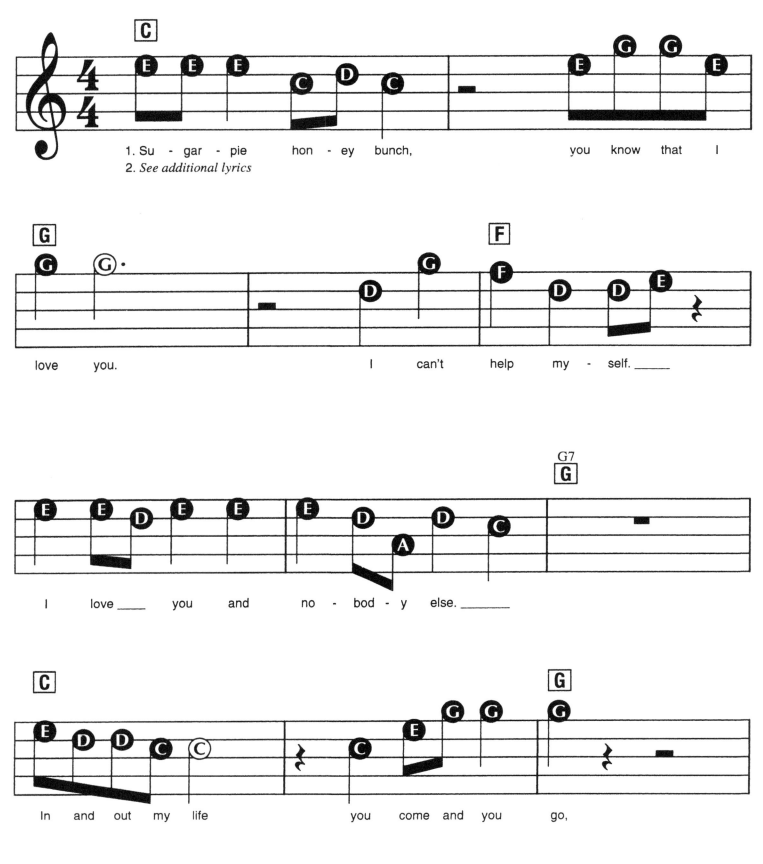

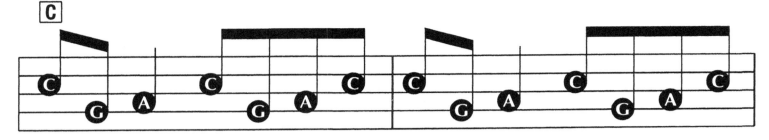

Instrumental

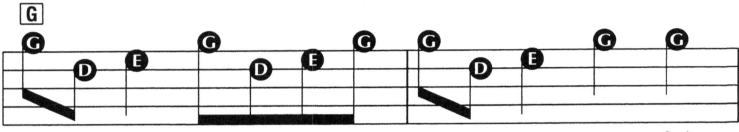

Can't

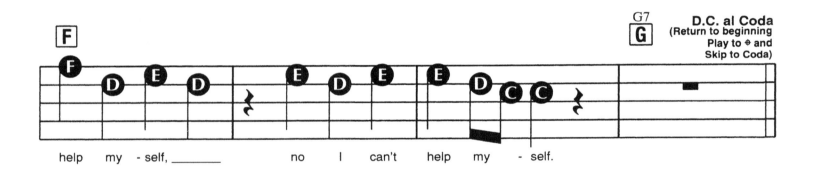

D.C. al Coda
(Return to beginning
Play to ⊕ and
Skip to Coda)

help my - self, _____ no I can't help my - self.

CODA

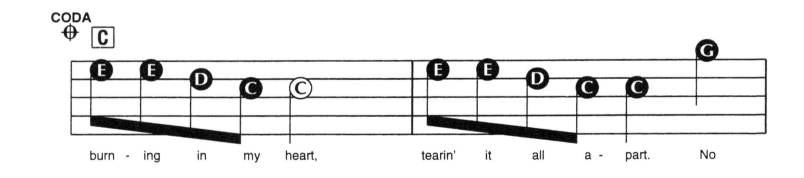

burn - ing in my heart, tearin' it all a - part. No

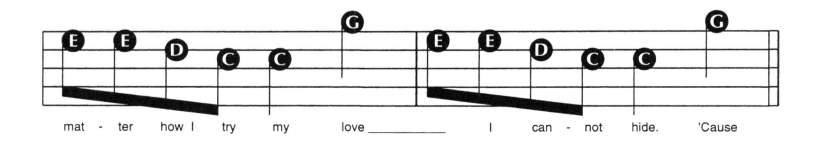

mat - ter how I try my love _____ I can - not hide. 'Cause

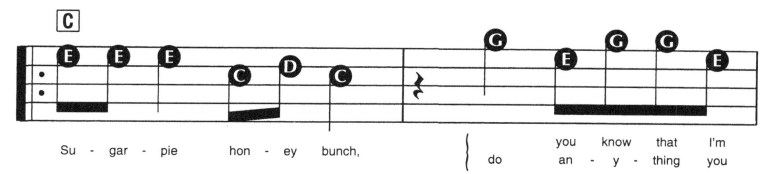

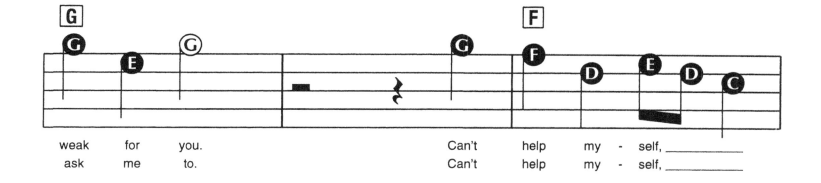

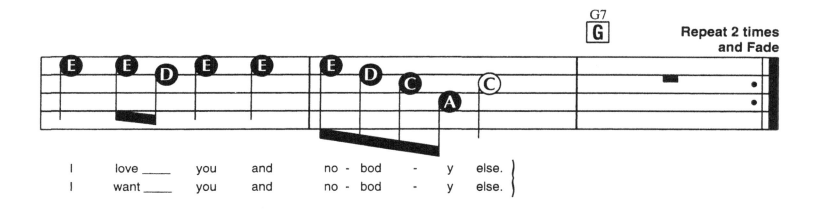

Additional Lyrics

2. Sugarpie honey bunch, I'm weaker than a man should be.
I can't help myself, I'm a fool in love you see.
Wanna tell you I don't love you, tell you that we're through, and I've tried.
But ev'ry time I see your face, I get all choked up inside.
I call your name, girl,
It starts the flame burning.

I Heard It Through the Grapevine

Registration 7
Rhythm: Rock or 8-Beat

Words and Music by Norman J. Whitfield
and Barrett Strong

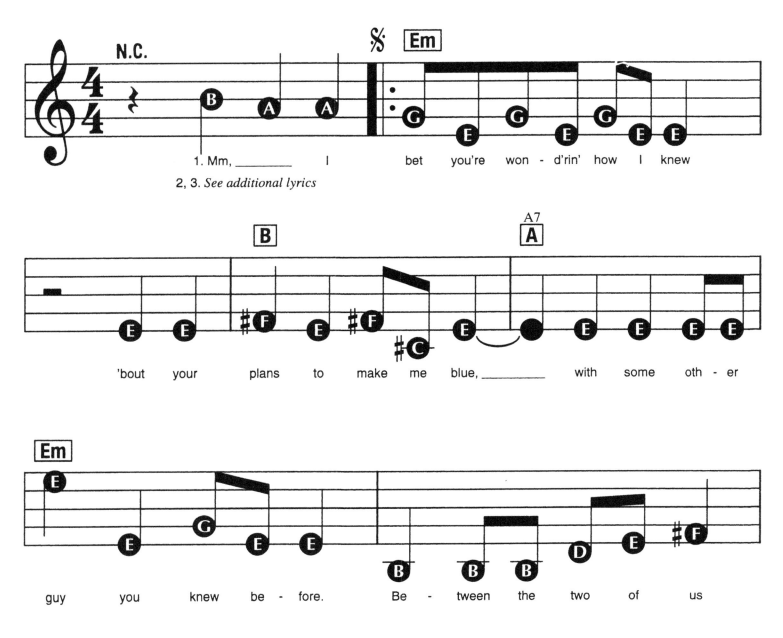

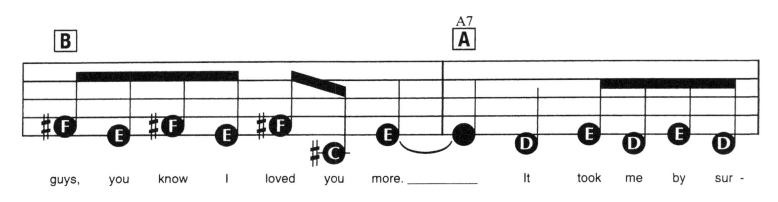

prise, _____ I must say, when I

found out yes - ter - day. _____ Don't you know that I heard

it through the grape - vine, not much _____

long - er would you be _____ mine. Uh huh,

heard it through the grape - vine. Oh, I'm just

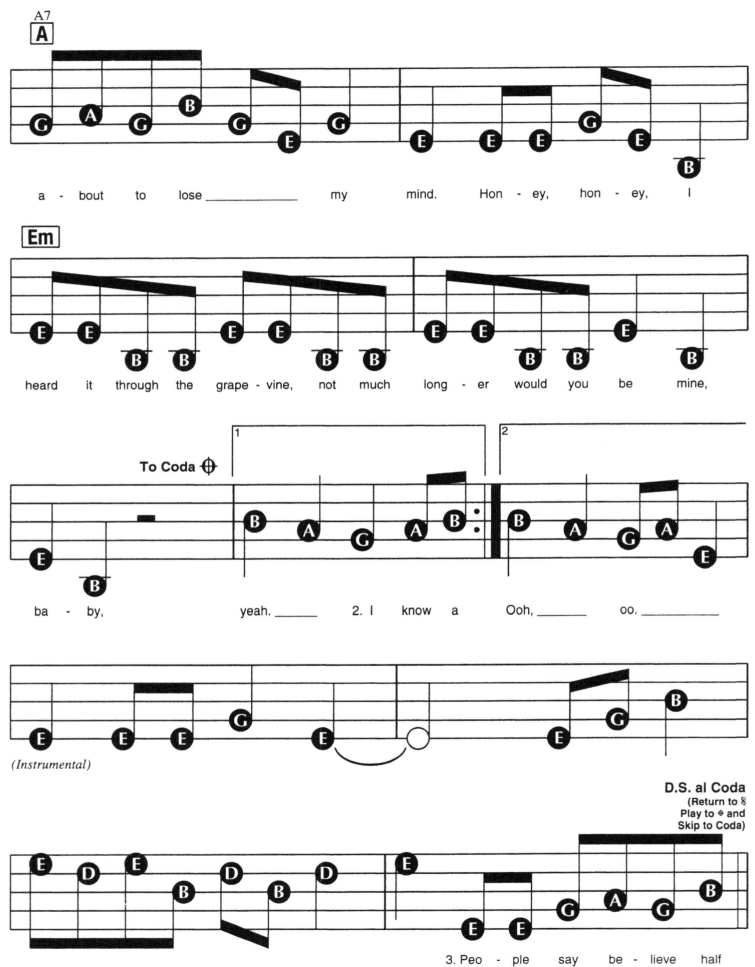

CODA

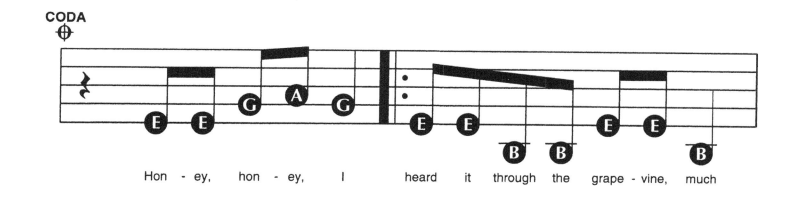

Hon - ey,   hon - ey,   I   heard   it   through   the   grape - vine,   much

Repeat and Fade

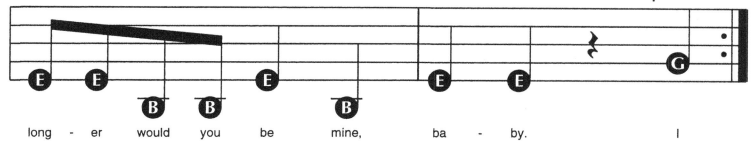

long - er   would   you   be   mine,   ba - by.   I

Additional Lyrics

2. I know a man ain't supposed to cry,
   but these tears I can't hold inside.
   Losin' you would end my life, you see,
   'cause you mean that much to me.
   You could have told me yourself
   that you loved someone else.
   Instead, I heard it through the grapevine,
   not much longer would you be mine.
   Oh, I heard it through the grapevine,
   and I'm just about to lose my mind.

3. People say believe half of what you see,
   oh, and none of what you hear.
   But I can't help but be confused.
   If it's true please tell me, dear.
   Do you plan to let me go
   for the other guy you loved before?

I Want You Back

Registration 4
Rhythm: R&B or 8 Beat

Words and Music by Freddie Perren,
Alphonso Mizell, Berry Gordy
and Deke Richards

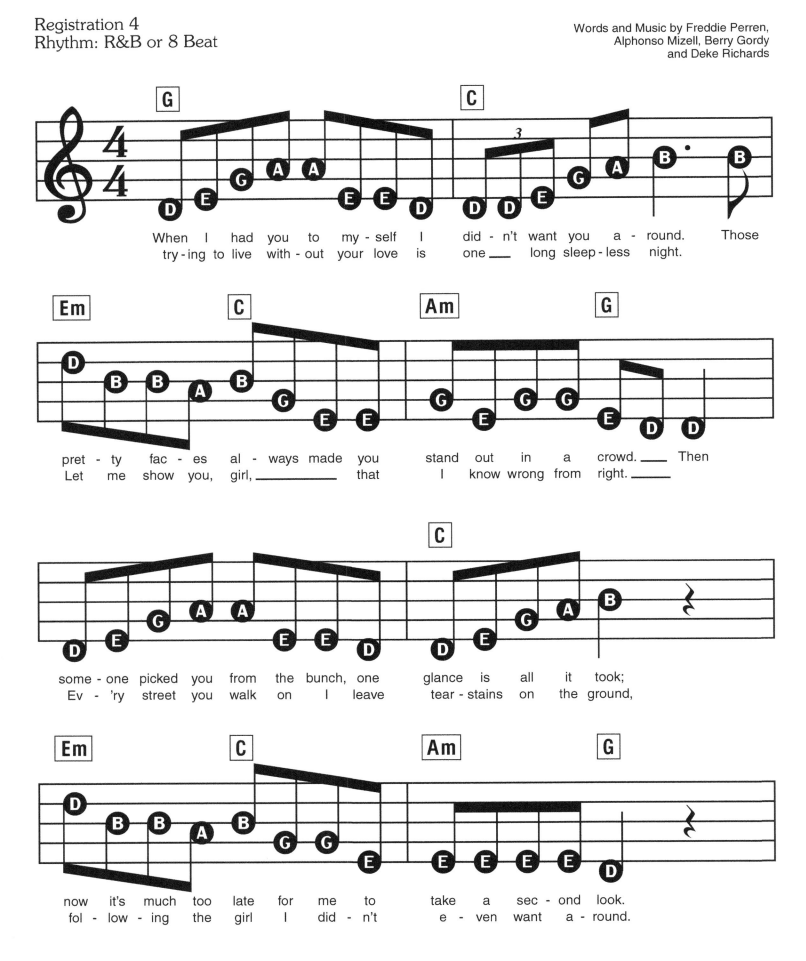

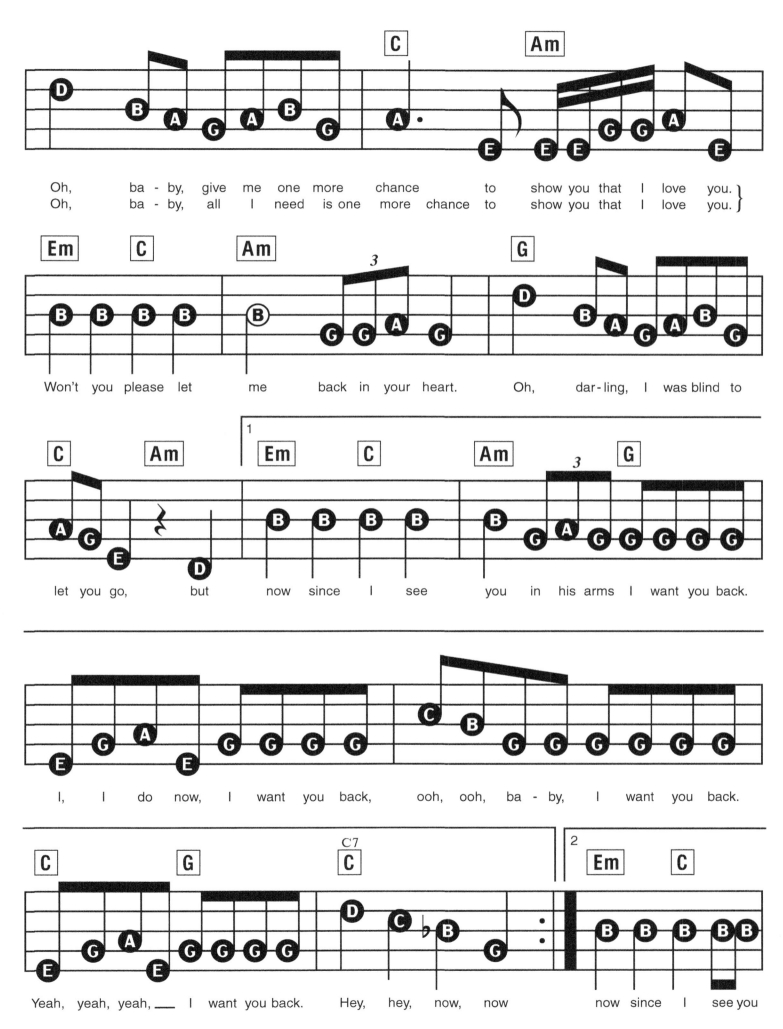

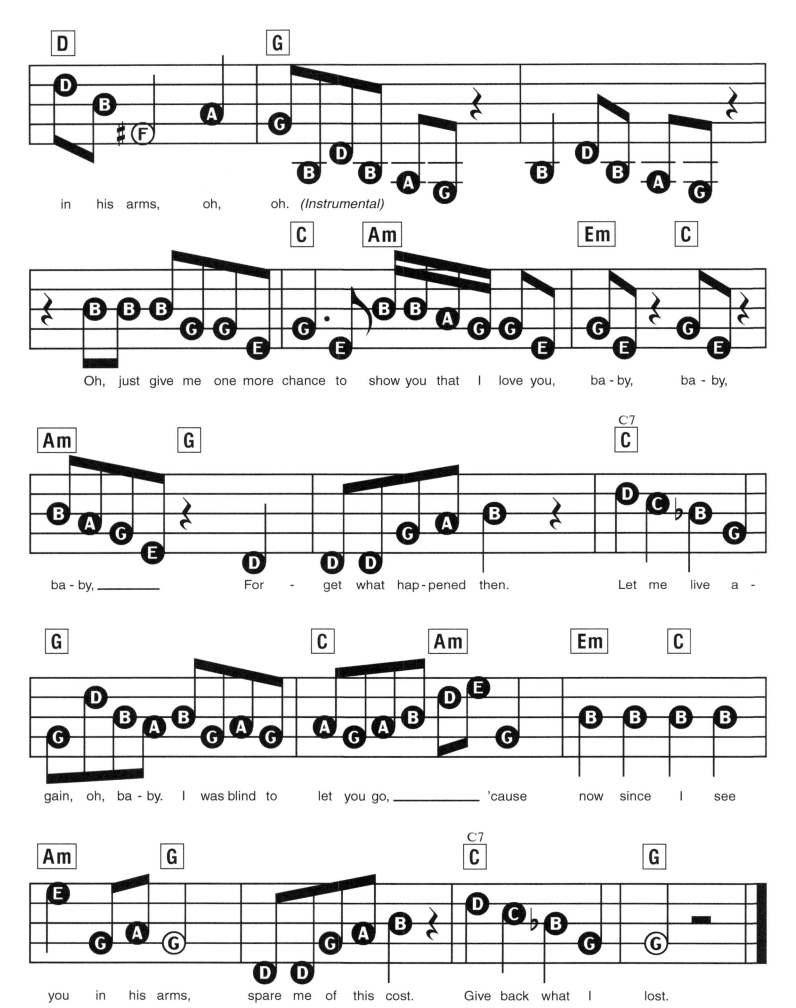

in his arms, oh, oh. *(Instrumental)*

Oh, just give me one more chance to show you that I love you, ba - by, ba - by,

ba - by, _____ For - get what hap - pened then. Let me live a -

gain, oh, ba - by. I was blind to let you go, _____ 'cause now since I see

you in his arms, spare me of this cost. Give back what I lost.

Let's Get It On

Registration 7
Rhythm: Rock or 8 Beat

Words and Music by Marvin Gaye
and Ed Townsend

I've been real - ly try - in', ba - by,

try - in' to hold _____ back this feel - in' for so _____ long. _____

And if you feel like I feel, _____ ba - by,

then come on, oh, come _____ on. Ooh, let's get it

62

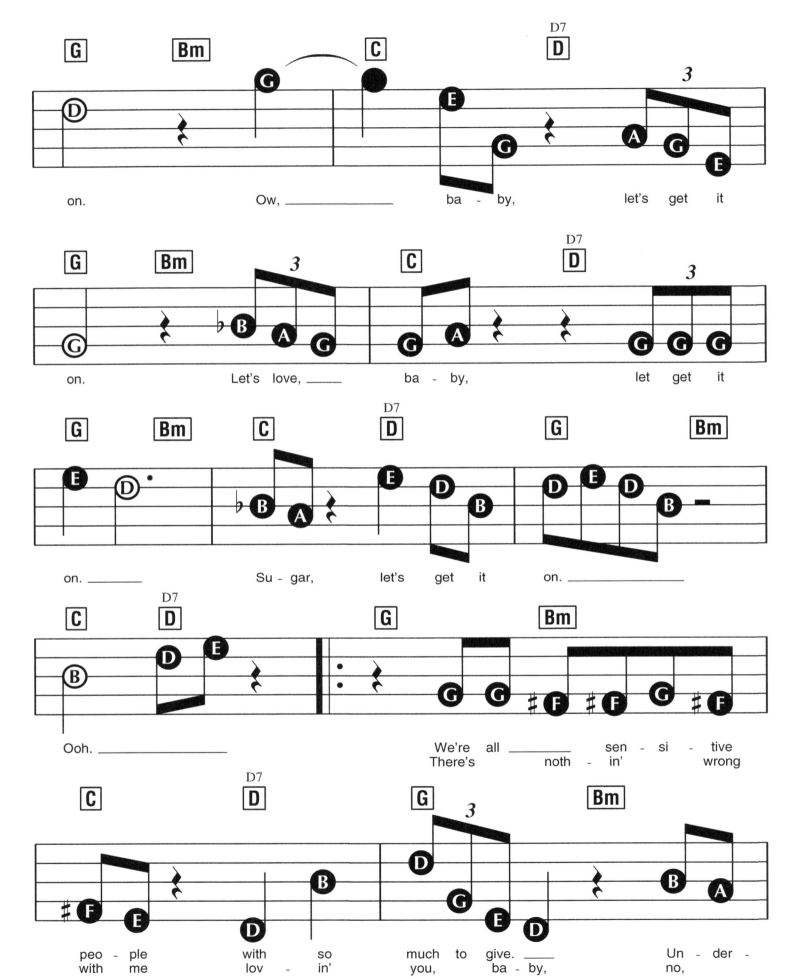

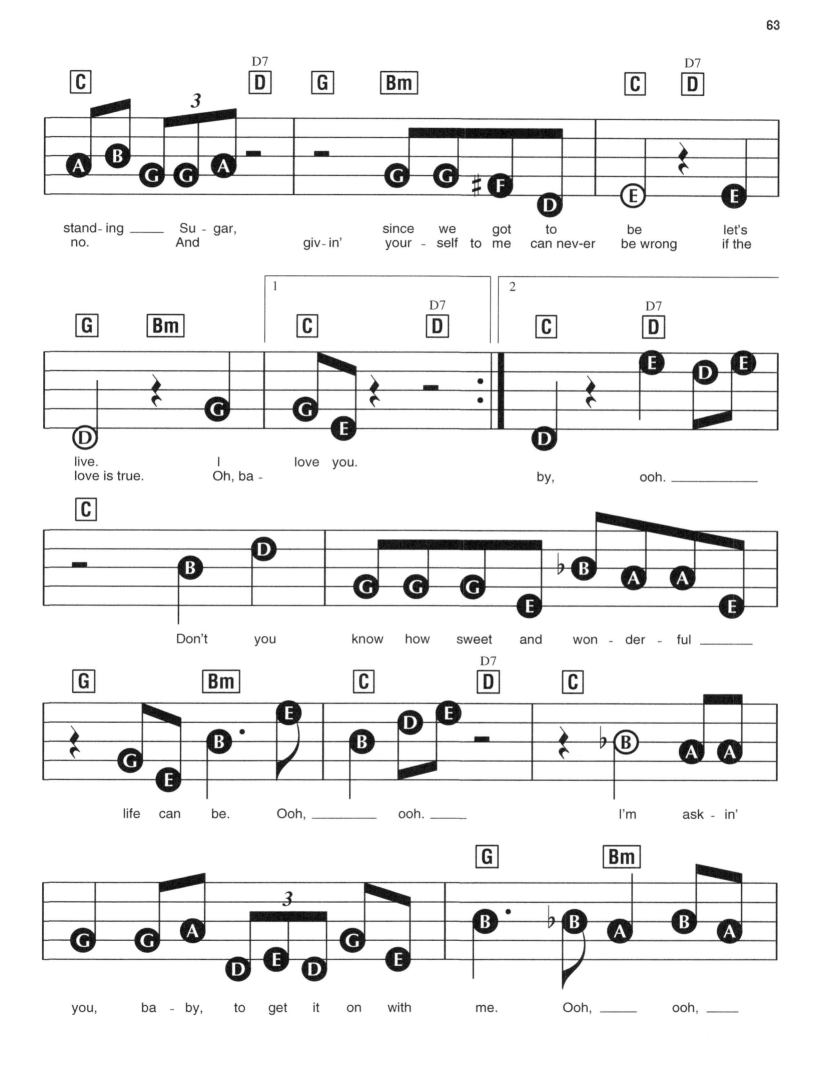

64

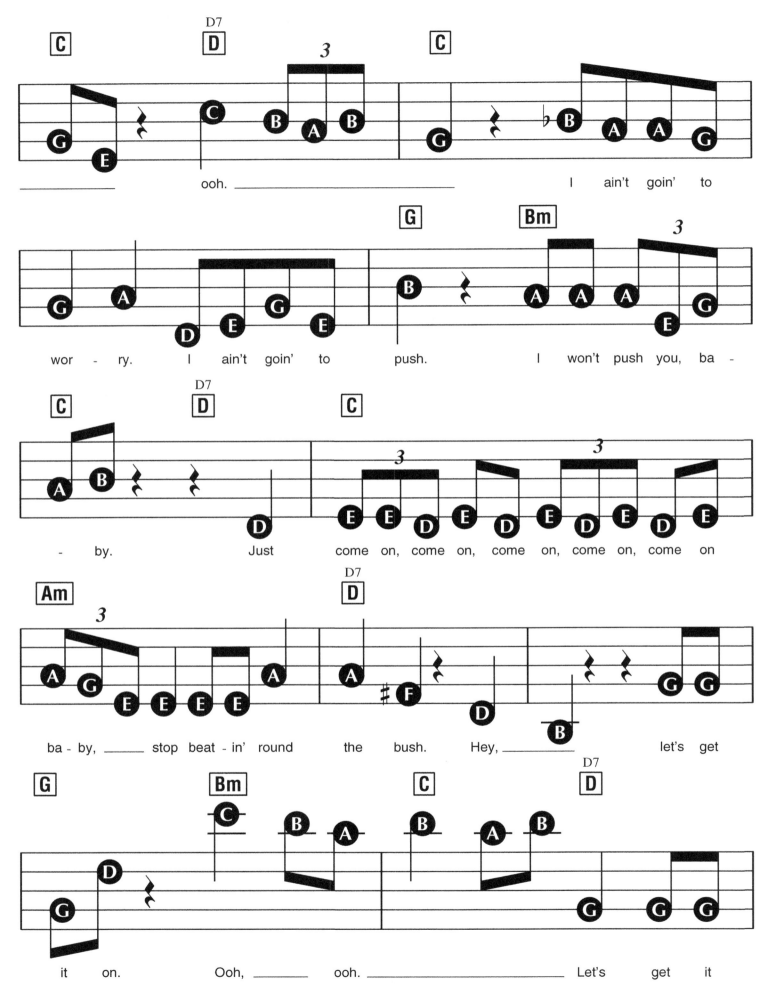

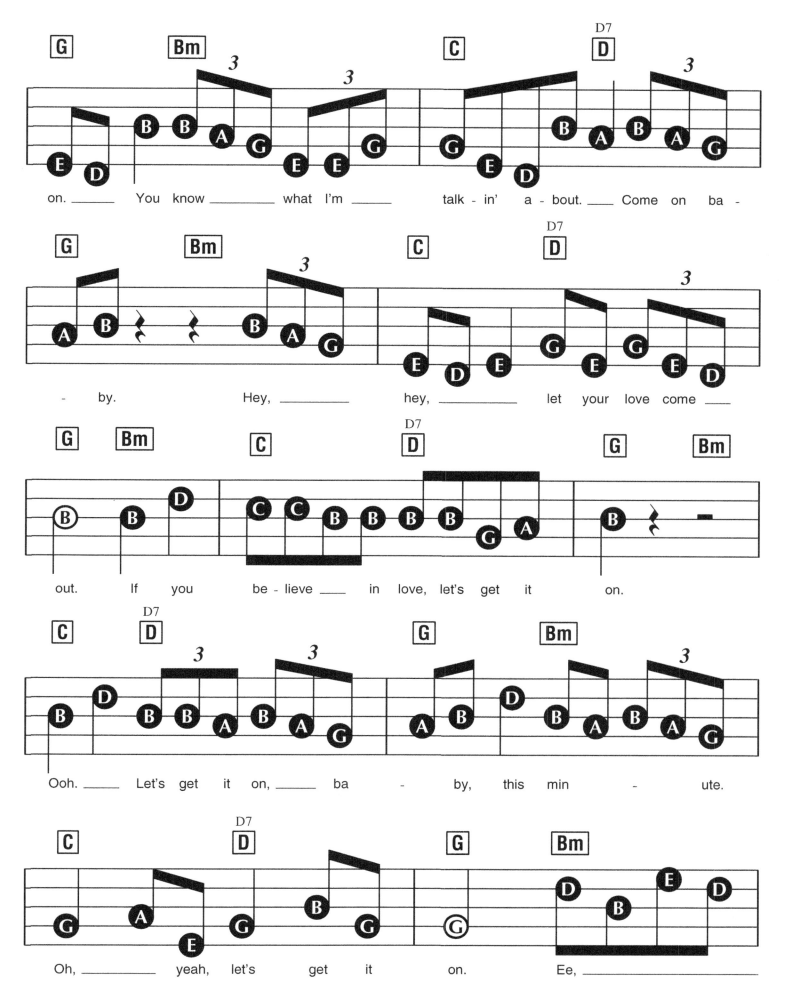

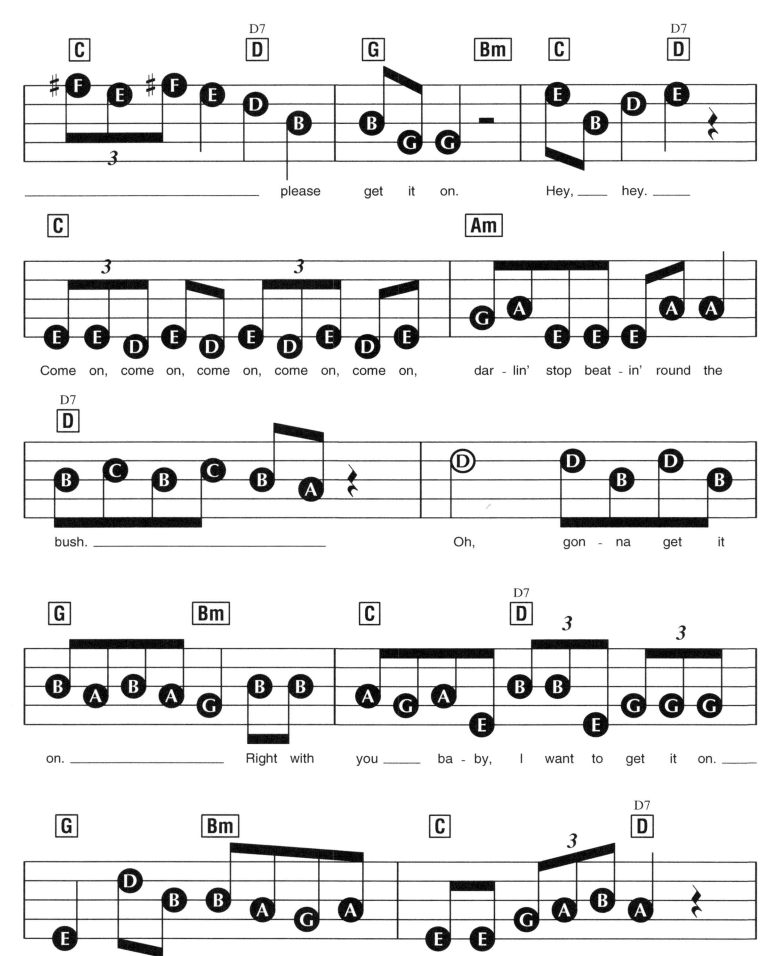

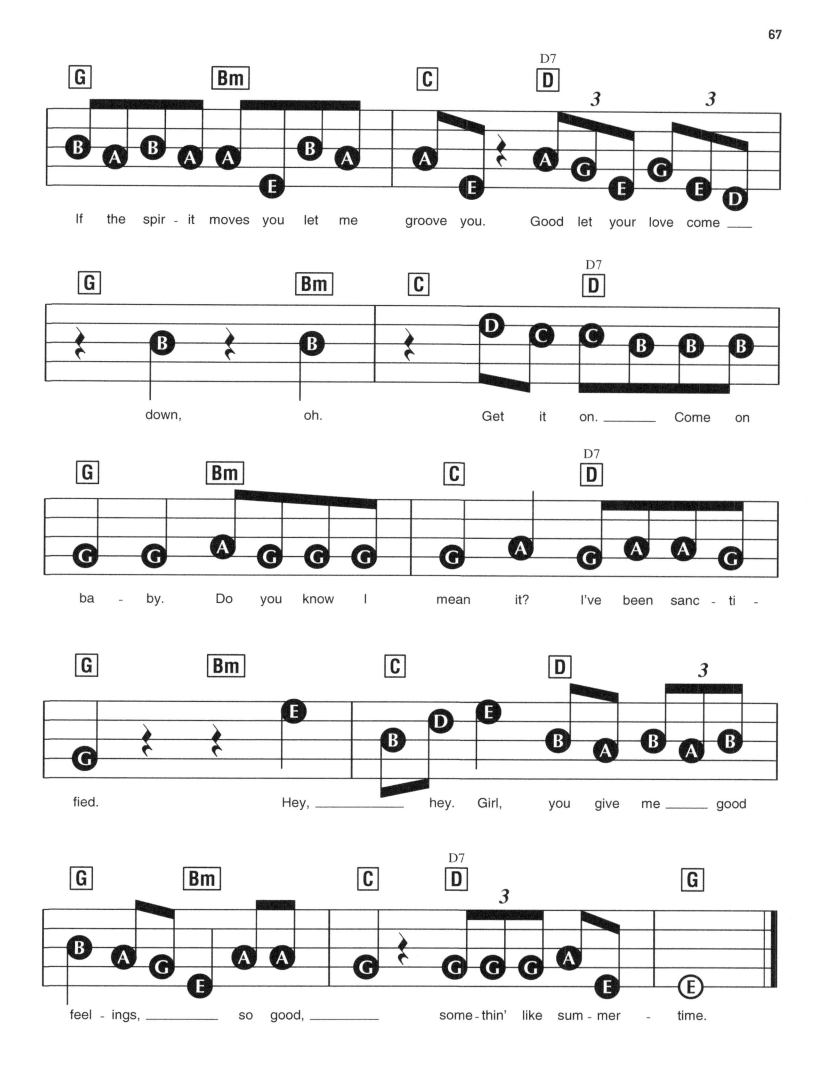

I'll Be There

Registration 9
Rhythm: Rock or 8-Beat

Words and Music by Berry Gordy, Hal Davis,
Willie Hutch and Bob West

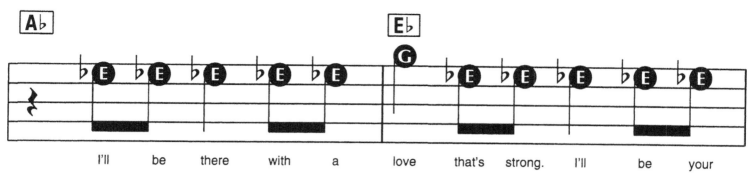

I'll be there with a love that's strong. I'll be your

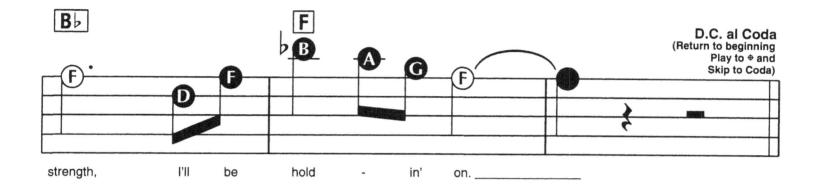

D.C. al Coda
(Return to beginning
Play to ⊕ and
Skip to Coda)

strength, I'll be hold - in' on. _____

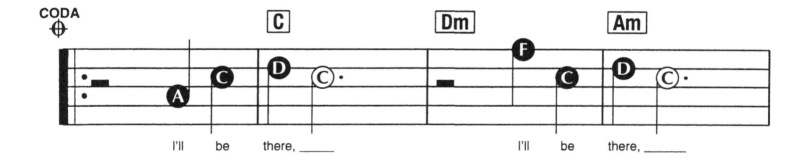

I'll be there, _____ I'll be there, _____

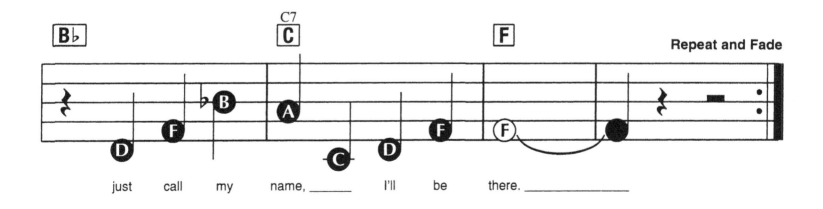

Repeat and Fade

just call my name, _____ I'll be there. _____

Additional Lyrics

3. Let me fill your heart with joy and laughter.
   Togetherness, girl, is all I'm after.
   Whenever you need me, I'll be there.

4. I'll be there to protect you
   With unselfish love that respects you.
   Just call my name, I'll be there.

Just My Imagination
(Running Away with Me)

Registration 3
Rhythm: Rock or 8-Beat

Words and Music by Norman J. Whitfield
and Barrett Strong

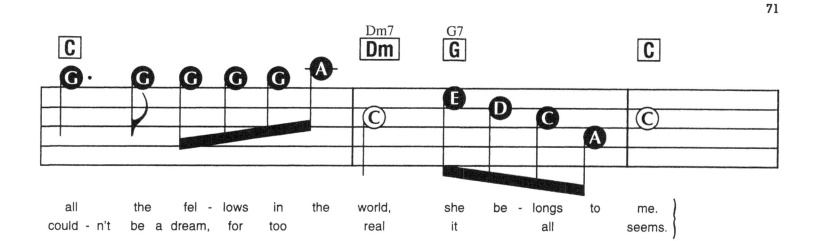

all the fel - lows in the world, she be - longs to me.
could - n't be a dream, for too real it all seems.

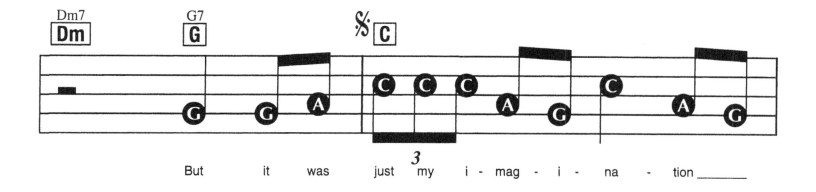

But it was just my i - mag - i - na - tion _____

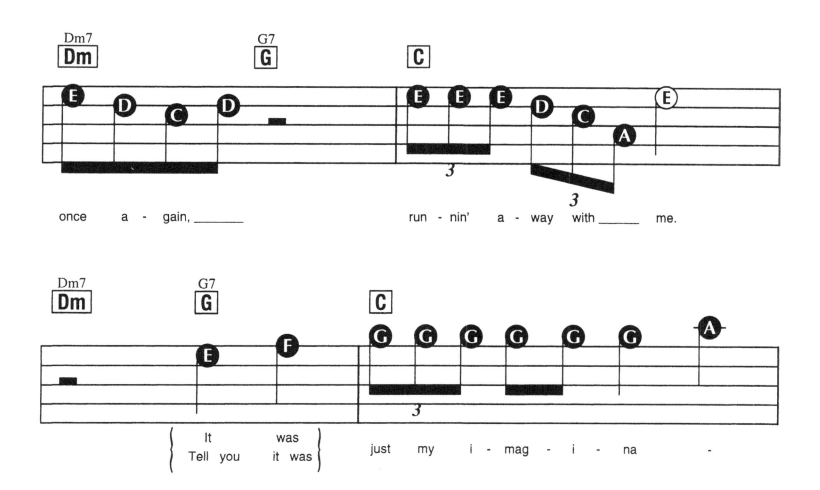

once a - gain, _____ run - nin' a - way with _____ me.

It was
Tell you it was

just my i - mag - i - na -

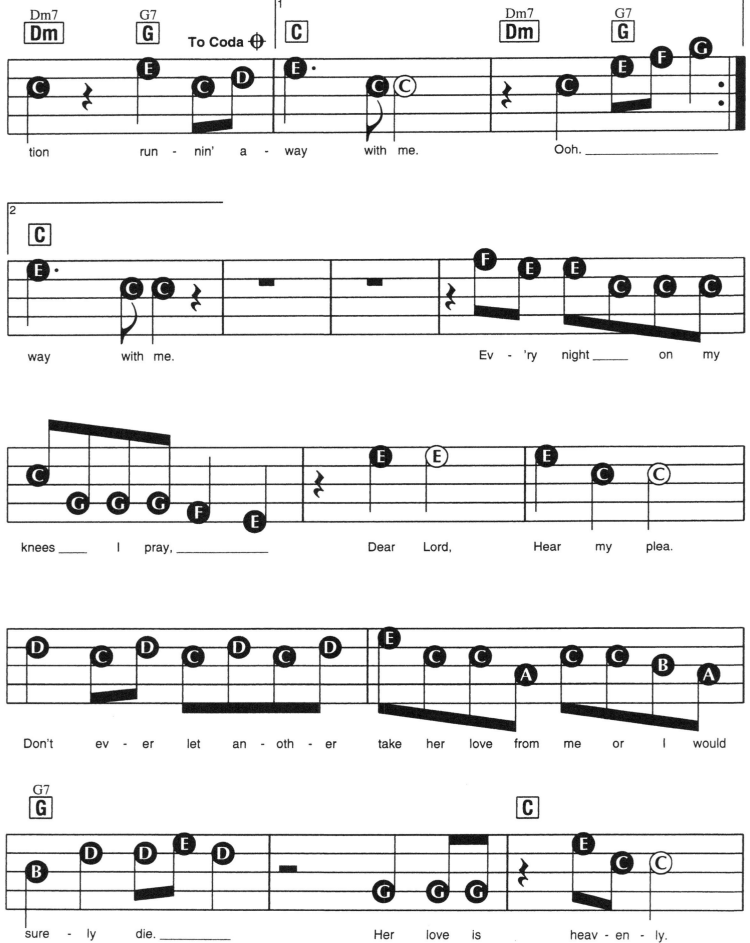

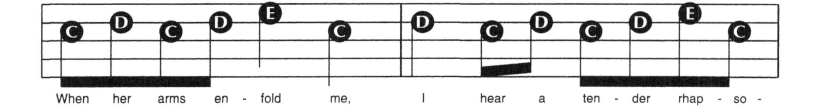

When her arms en - fold me, I hear a ten - der rhap - so -

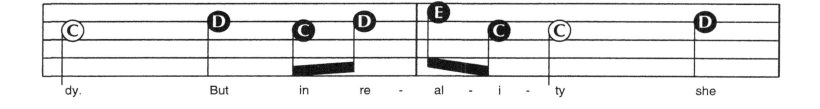

dy. But in re - al - i - ty she

D.S. al Coda
(Return to 𝄋
Play to ⊕ and
Skip to Coda)

CODA
⊕
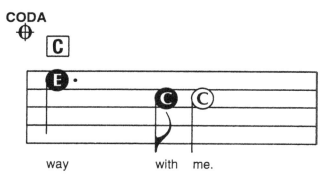

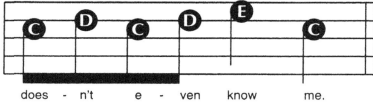

does - n't e - ven know me.

way with me.

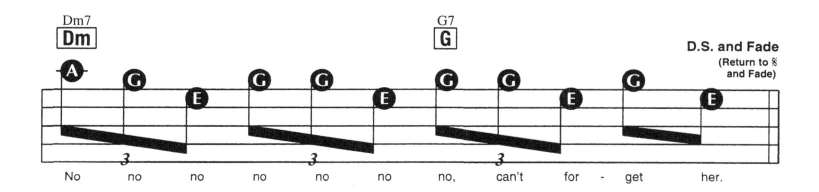

No no no no no no no, can't for - get her.

Money
(That's What I Want)

Registration 5
Rhythm: Rock 'n' Roll

Words and Music by Berry Gordy
and Janie Bradford

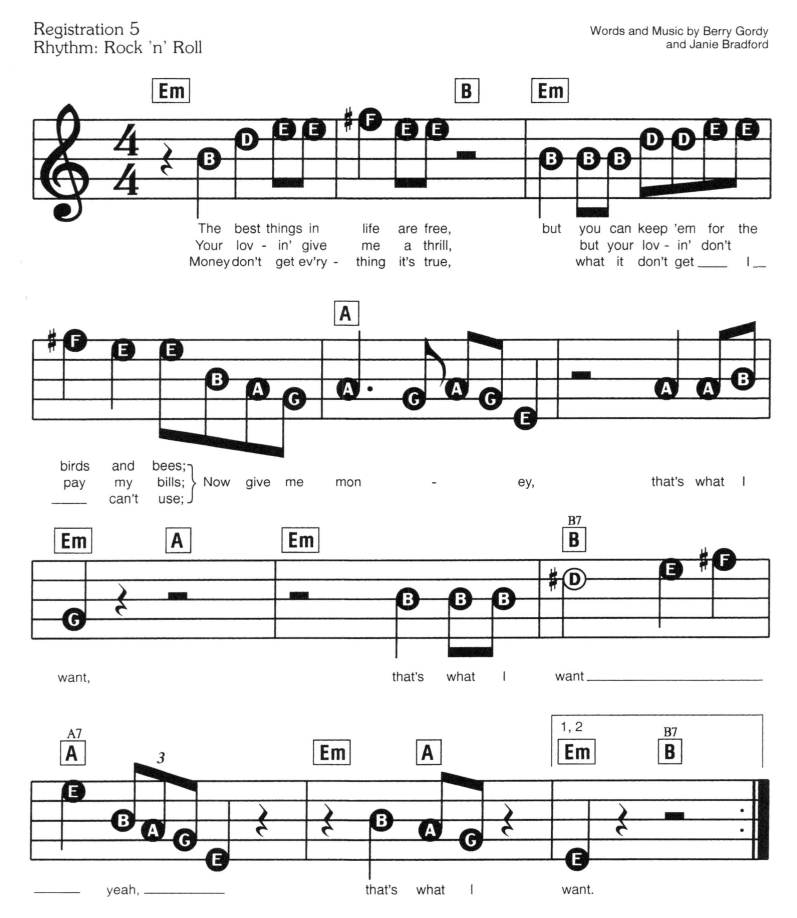

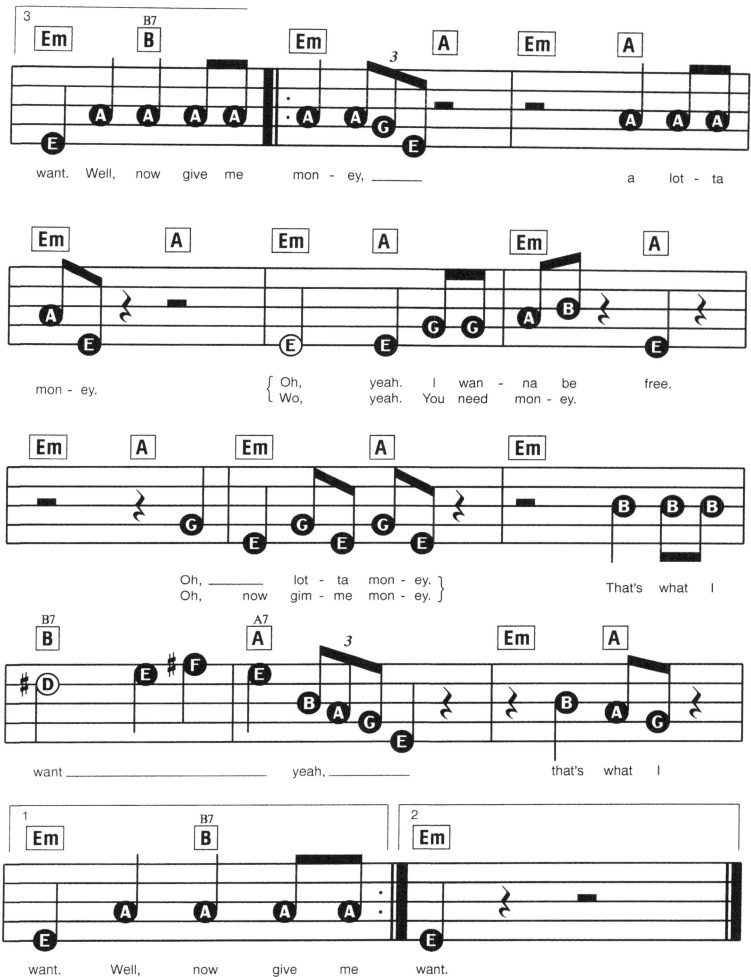

My Girl

Registration 4
Rhythm: Rock or 8-Beat

Words and Music by William "Smokey" Robinson
and Ronald White

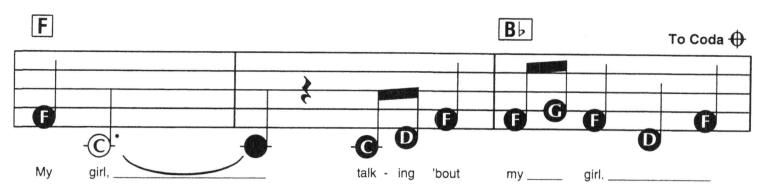

My girl, _____ talk - ing 'bout my _____ girl. _____

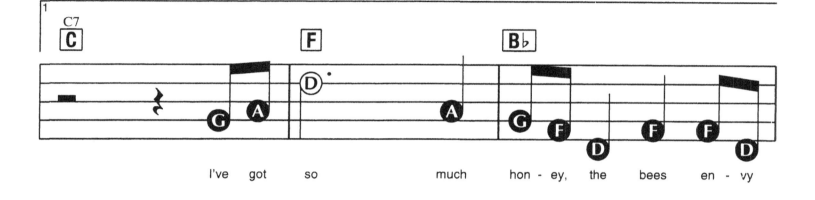

I've got so much hon - ey, the bees en - vy

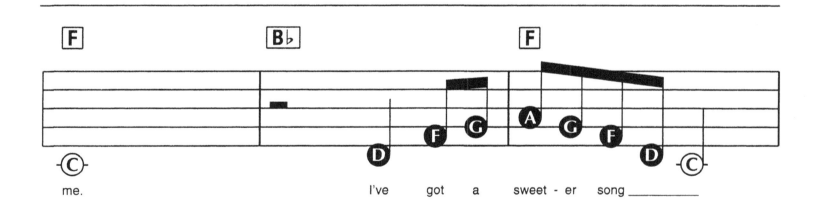

me. I've got a sweet - er song _____

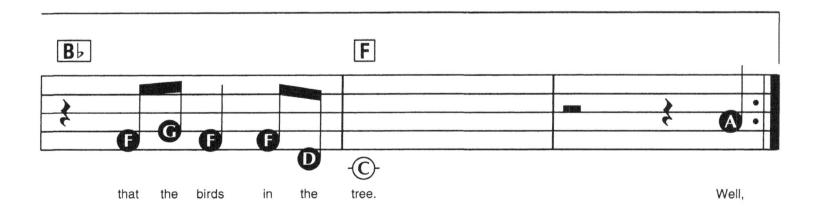

that the birds in the tree. Well,

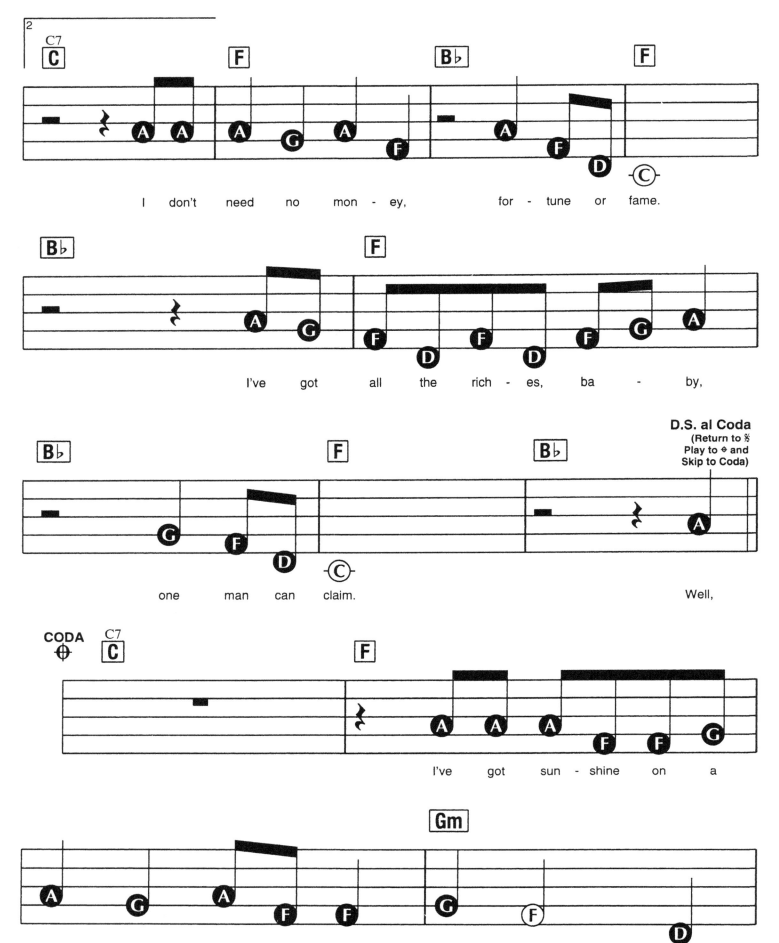

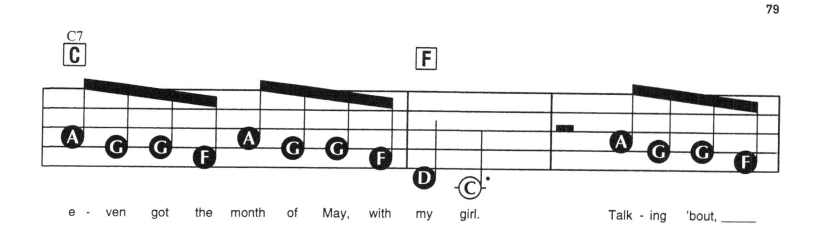

e - ven got the month of May, with my girl. Talk - ing 'bout, _____

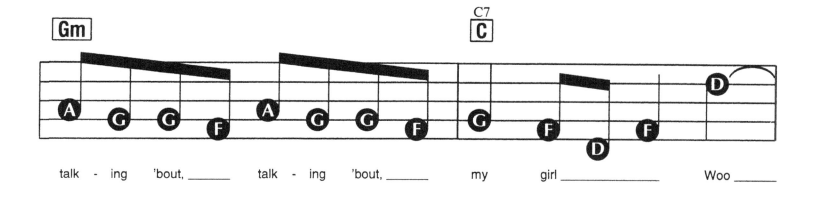

talk - ing 'bout, _____ talk - ing 'bout, _____ my girl _____ Woo _____

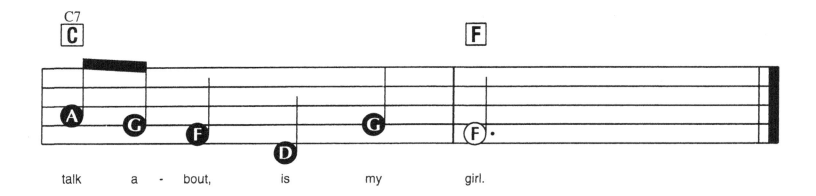

_____ my girl. That's all I can

talk a - bout, is my girl.

My Guy

Registration 8
Rhythm: Swing or Shuffle

Words and Music by
William "Smokey" Robinson

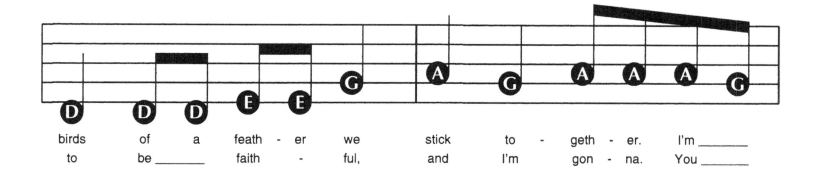

birds of a feath - er we stick to - geth - er. I'm _____
to be _____ faith - ful, and I'm gon - na. You _____

C

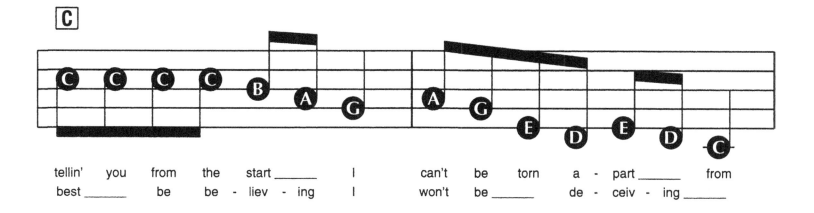

tellin' you from the start _____ I can't be torn a - part _____ from
best _____ be be - liev - ing I won't be _____ de - ceiv - ing _____

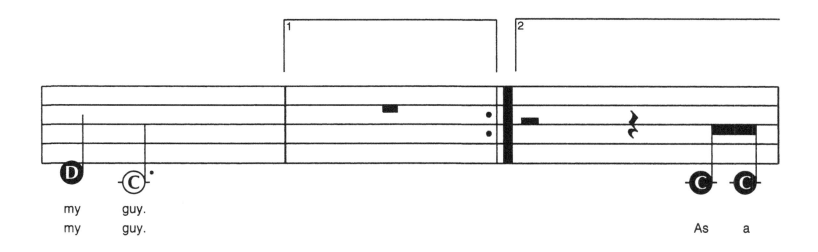

my guy.
my guy.   As a

G7
G

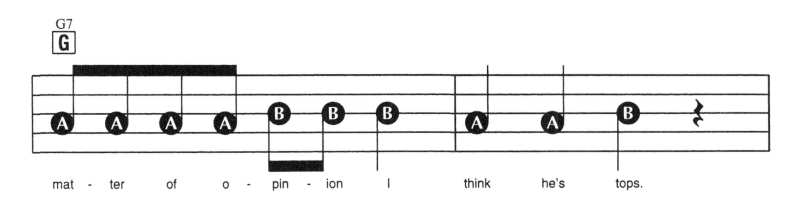

mat - ter of o - pin - ion I think he's tops.

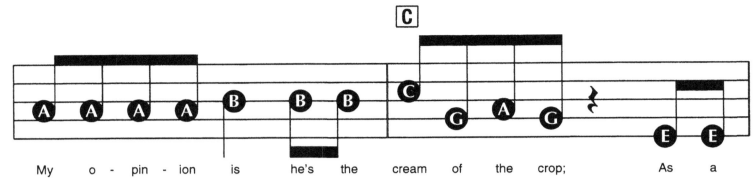

My o - pin - ion is he's the cream of the crop; As a

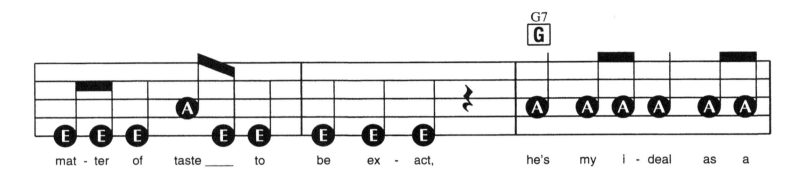

mat - ter of taste ____ to be ex - act, he's my i - deal as a

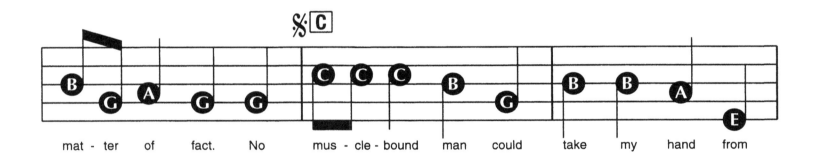

mat - ter of fact. No mus - cle - bound man could take my hand from

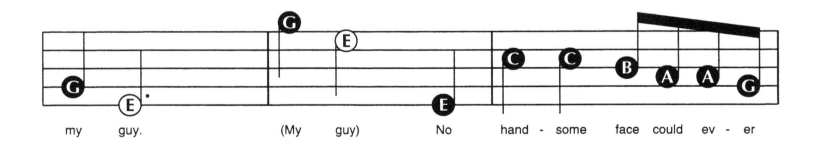

my guy. (My guy) No hand - some face could ev - er

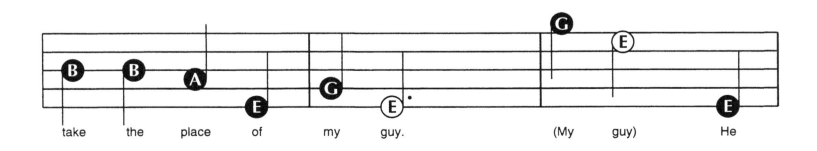

take the place of my guy. (My guy) He

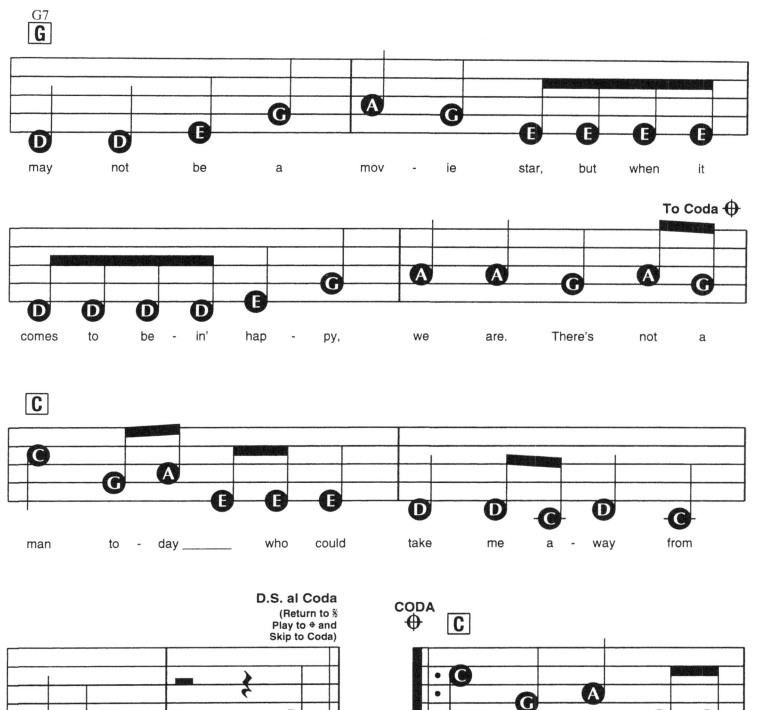

may not be a mov - ie star, but when it

comes to be - in' hap - py, we are. There's not a

man to - day _____ who could take me a - way from

D.S. al Coda
(Return to %
Play to ⊕ and
Skip to Coda)

CODA

my guy. No

man to - day who could

Repeat and Fade

take me a - way from my guy. There's not a

Never Can Say Goodbye

Registration 9
Rhythm: Disco or 16-Beat

Words and Music by
Clifton Davis

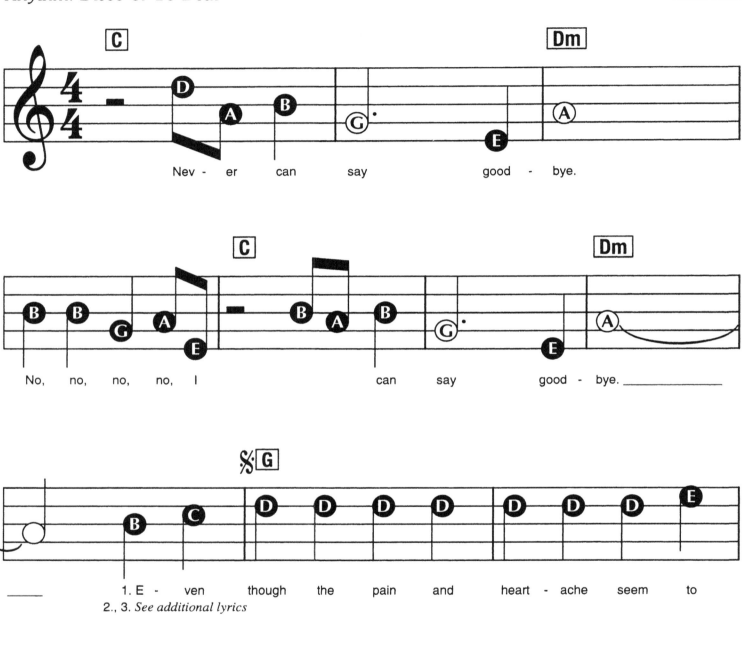

Nev - er can say good - bye.

No, no, no, no, I can say good - bye. _____

_____ 1. E - ven though the pain and heart - ache seem to
2., 3. *See additional lyrics*

fol - low me where - ev - er I go, though I tried and tried to

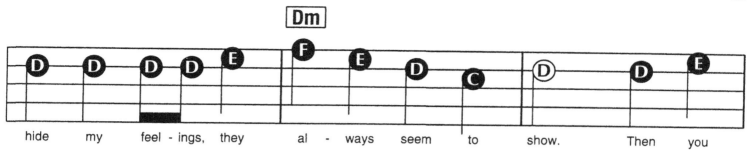

hide my feel - ings, they al - ways seem to show. Then you

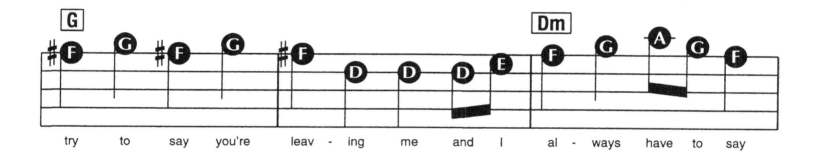

try to say you're leav - ing me and I al - ways have to say

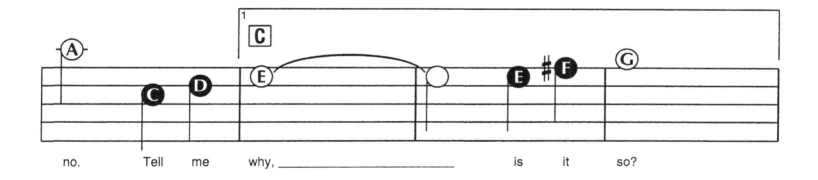

no. Tell me why, _____ is it so?

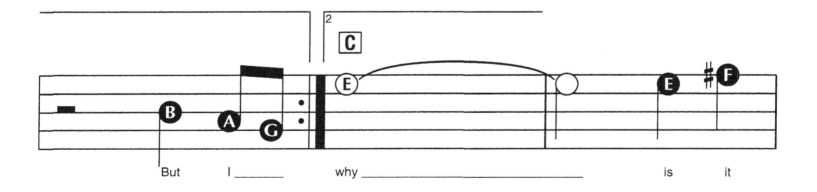

But I _____ why _____ is it

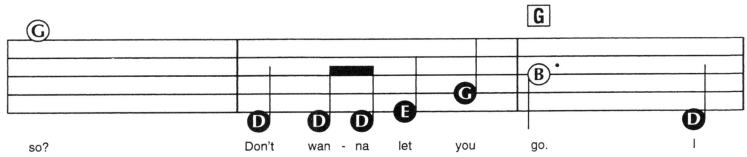

so?   Don't wan - na let you go.   I

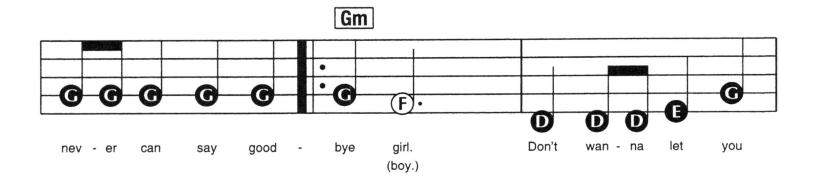

nev - er can say good - bye girl.   Don't wan - na let you
(boy.)

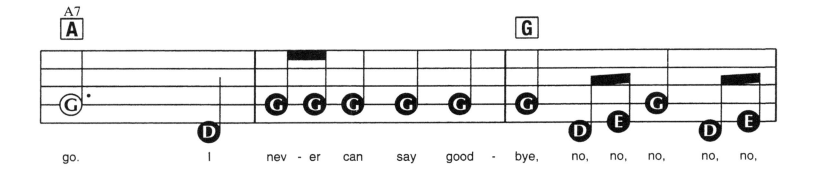

go.   I nev - er can say good - bye, no, no, no, no, no,

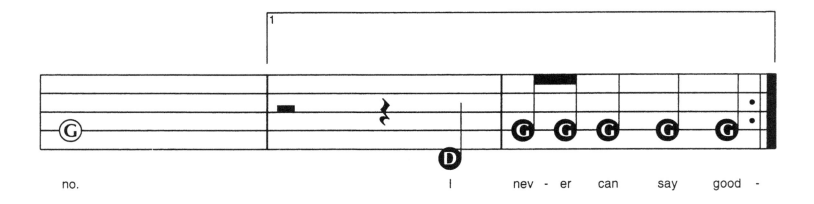

no.   I nev - er can say good -

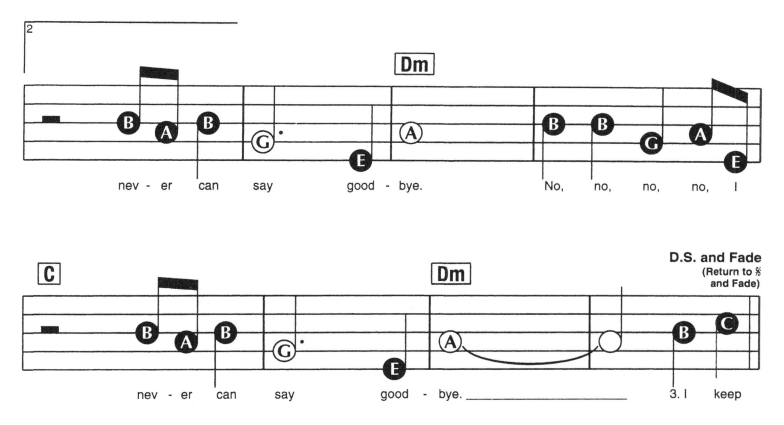

Additional Lyrics

2. Ev'ry time I think I've had enough and start heading for the door,
   there's very strange vibrations, piercing me right to the core. It says
   turn around, you fool, you know you love her more and more.

3. I keep thinkin' that our problems soon are all gonna work out,
   but there's that same unhappy feelin', there's that anguish, there's that
   doubt. It's that same old dizzy hang-up can't do with you or without.

Ooo Baby Baby

Registration 1
Rhythm: Rock or 8 Beat

Words and Music by William "Smokey" Robinson
and Warren Moore

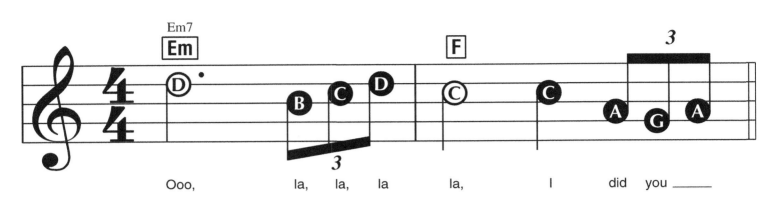

Ooo, la, la, la la, I did you ____

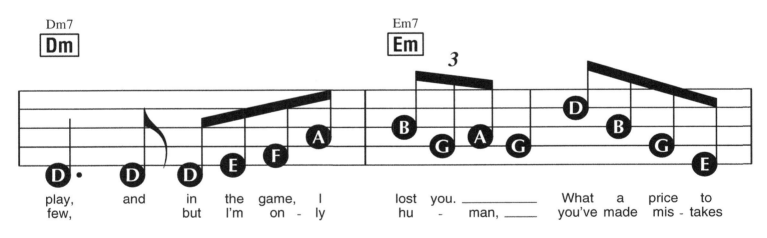

wrong, ____ my heart ____ went out to
takes, ____ I know ____ I've made to a

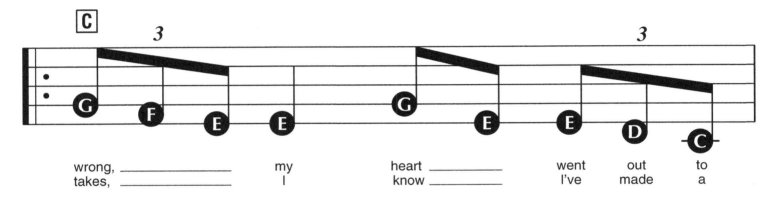

play, and in the game, I lost you. ____ What a price to
few, but I'm on - ly hu - man, ____ you've made mis - takes

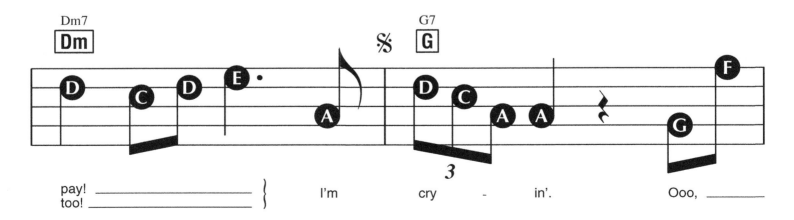

pay! ____ I'm cry - in'. Ooo, ____
too! ____

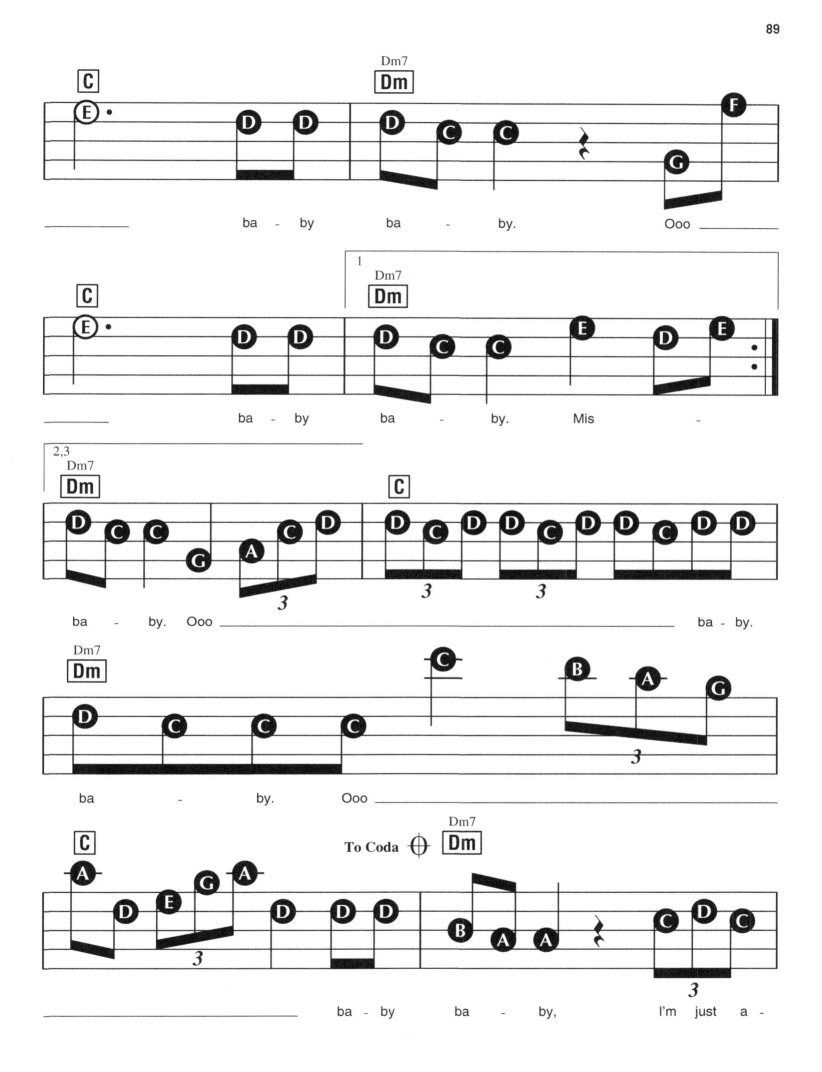

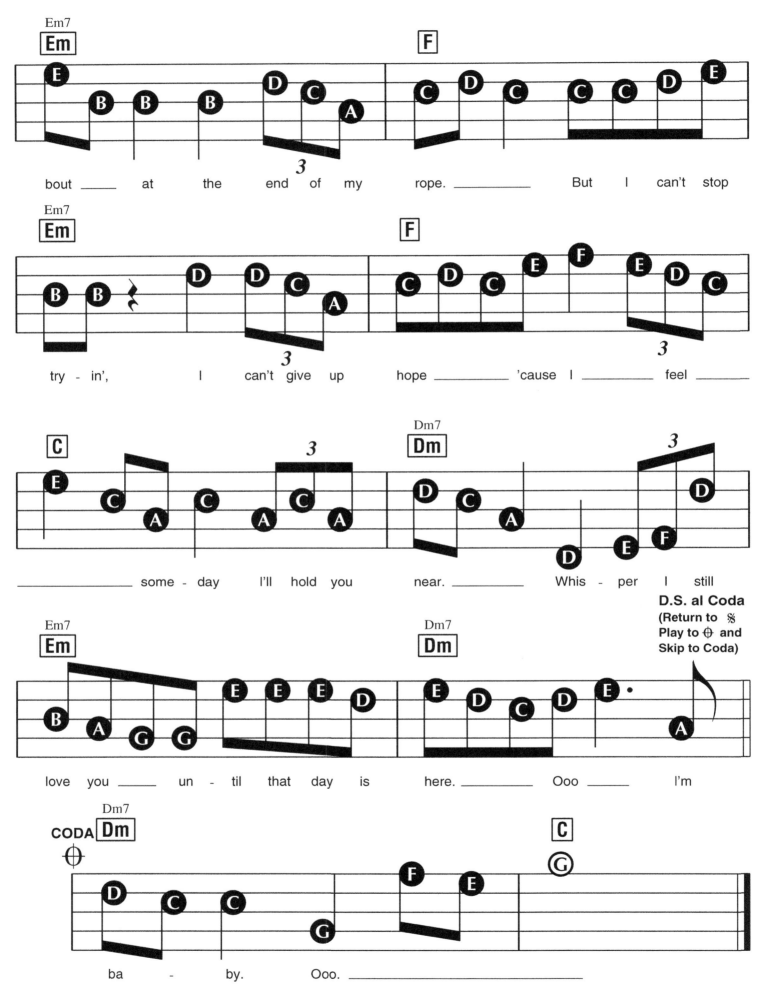

Reach Out, I'll Be There

Registration 9
Rhythm: Rock or 8-Beat

Words and Music by Brian Holland,
Lamont Dozier and Edward Holland

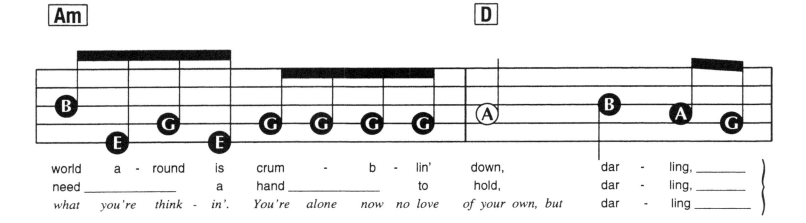

Am ... **D**

world	a - round	is	crum - b - lin'	down,	dar - ling, _____
need _____	a	hand _____	to	hold,	dar - ling, _____
what you're think - in'.	*You're alone*	*now no love*	*of your own, but*	*dar - ling _____*

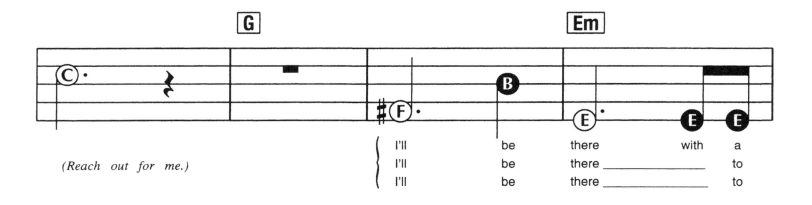

G ... **B**

reach out. *(Come on girl. reach on out for me.)* Reach out.

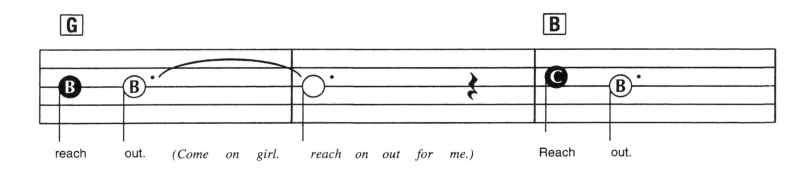

G ... **Em**

(Reach out for me.)

I'll	be	there	with	a
I'll	be	there _____	to
I'll	be	there _____	to

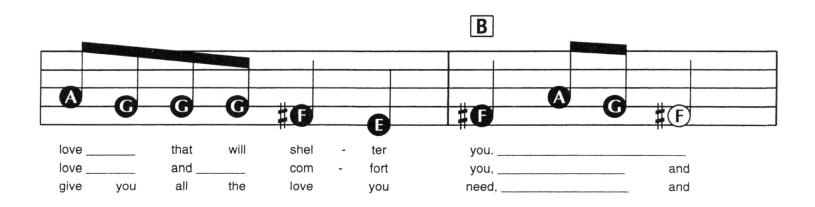

B

love _____	that	will	shel - ter	you. _____
love _____	and _____	com - fort	you, _____	and
give you	all	the	love you	need, _____	and

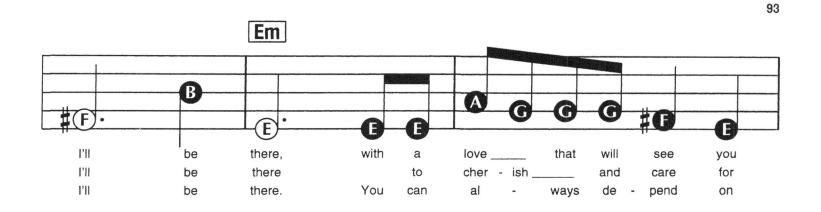

I'll be there, with a love ____ that will see you
I'll be there to cher - ish ____ and care for
I'll be there. You can al - ways de - pend on

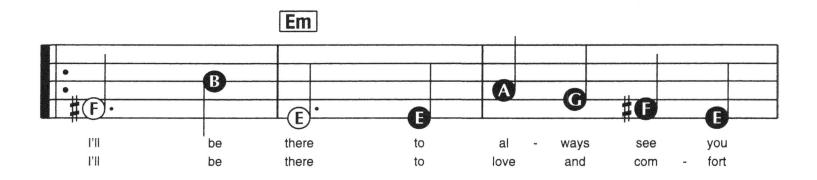

through. _____
you. _____
me. _____

When you feel

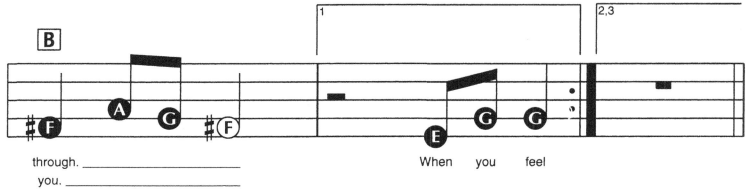

I'll be there to al - ways see you
I'll be there to love and com - fort

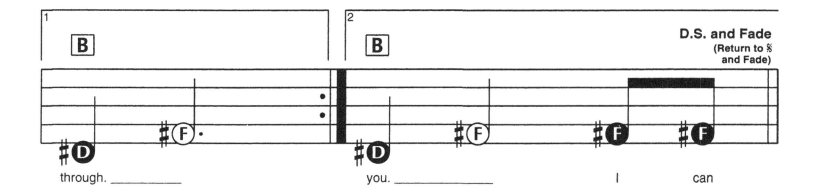

through. _____

you. _____

D.S. and Fade
(Return to 𝄋
and Fade)

I can

Papa Was a Rollin' Stone

Registration 9
Rhythm: Rock or 8-Beat

Words and Music by Norman Whitfield
and Barrett Strong

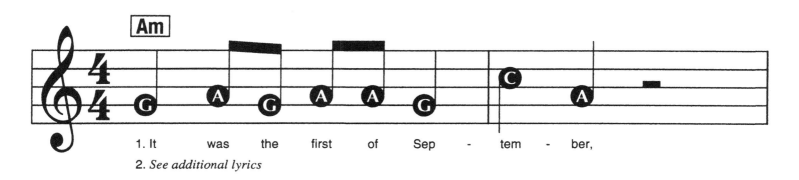

1. It was the first of Sep - tem - ber,
2. *See additional lyrics*

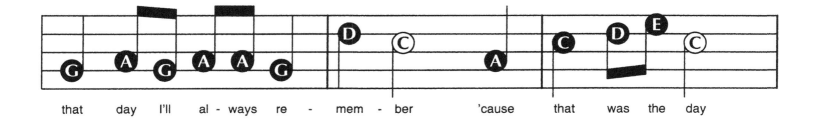

that day I'll al - ways re - mem - ber 'cause that was the day

that my dad - dy died. I nev - er got a chance to

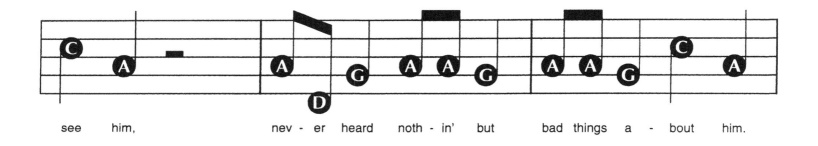

see him, nev - er heard noth - in' but bad things a - bout him.

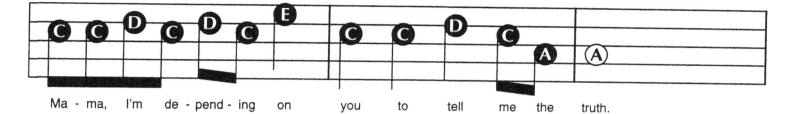

Ma - ma, I'm de - pend - ing on you to tell me the truth.

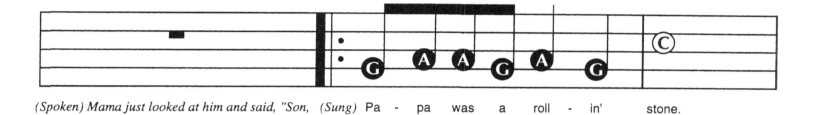

(Spoken) Mama just looked at him and said, "Son, (Sung) Pa - pa was a roll - in' stone.

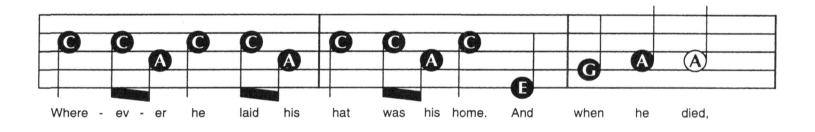

Where - ev - er he laid his hat was his home. And when he died,

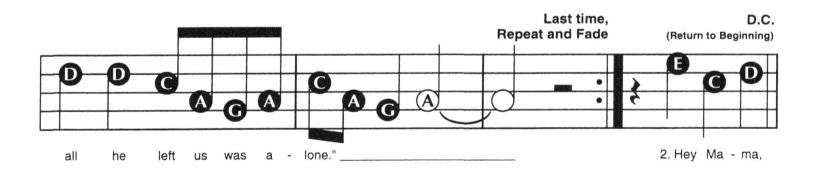

Last time, Repeat and Fade

D.C. (Return to Beginning)

all he left us was a - lone." _____ 2. Hey Ma - ma,

Additional Lyrics

2. Hey, Mama, I heard Papa call himself a jack of all trades.
Tell me, is that what sent Papa to an early grave?
Folks say Papa would beg, borrow or steal to pay his bills.
Hey, Mama, folks say Papa was never much on thinkin',
Spend most of his time chasin' women and drinkin'!
Mama, I'm depending on you to tell me the truth.
(Spoken:) Mama just hung her head and said, "Son, . . .

A Place in the Sun

Registration 8
Rhythm: Rock or Latin

Words and Music by Ronald Miller
and Bryan Wells

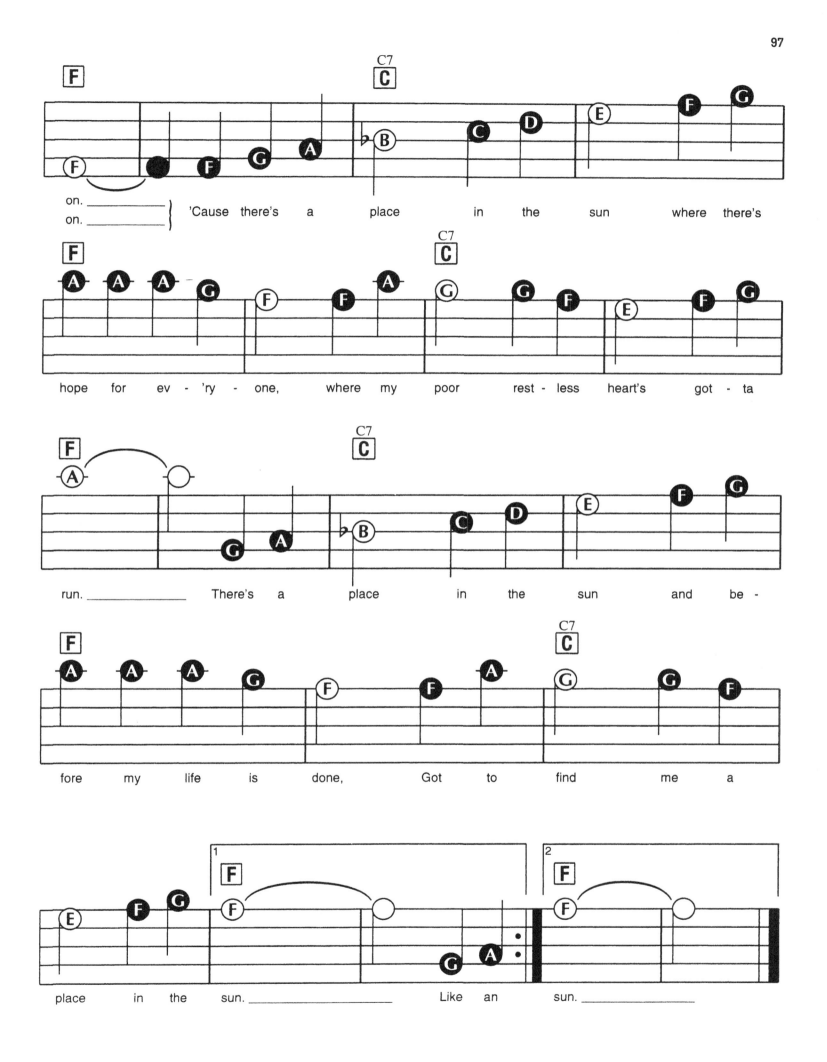

Reach Out and Touch
(Somebody's Hand)

Registration 4
Rhythm: Waltz

Words and Music by Nickolas Ashford
and Valerie Simpson

Shop Around

Registration 4
Rhythm: Rock or 8-Beat

Words and Music by Berry Gordy
and William "Smokey" Robinson

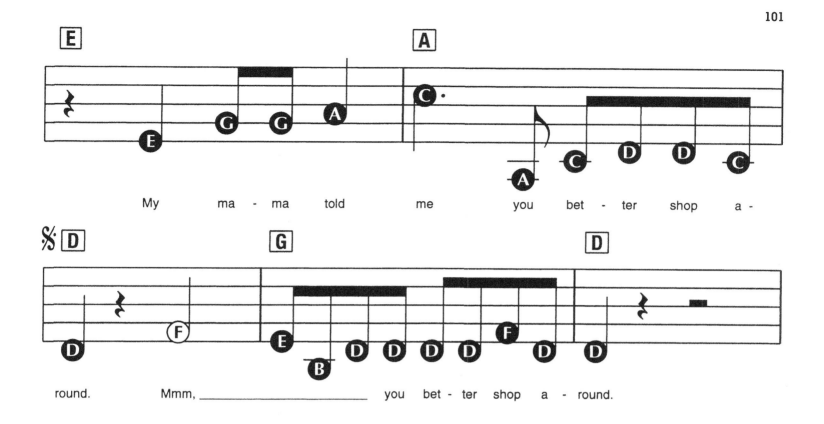

My ma - ma told me you bet - ter shop a -

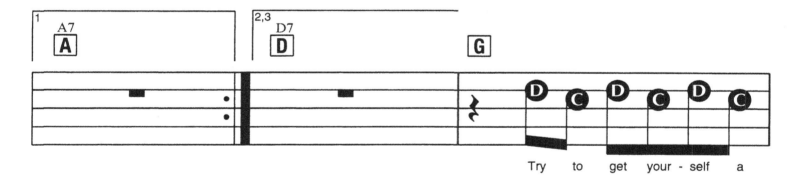

round. Mmm, _____ you bet - ter shop a - round.

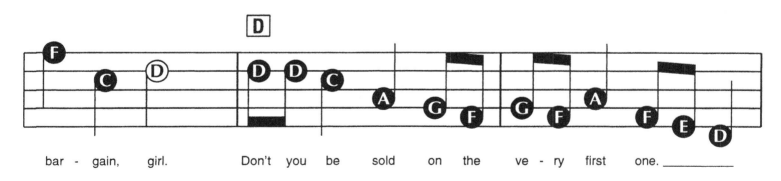

Try to get your - self a

bar - gain, girl. Don't you be sold on the ve - ry first one. _____

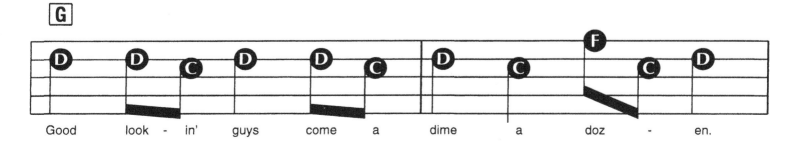

Good look - in' guys come a dime a doz - en.

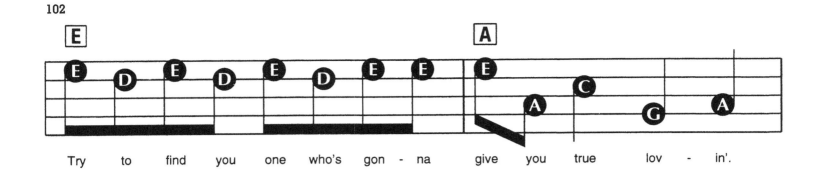

Try to find you one who's gon - na give you true lov - in'.

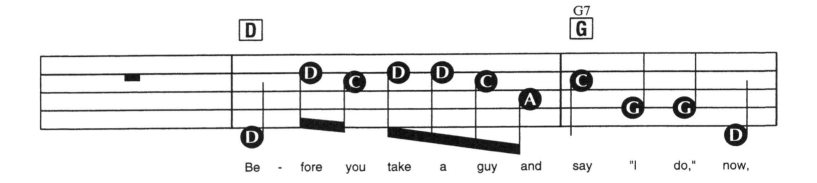

Be - fore you take a guy and say "I do," now,

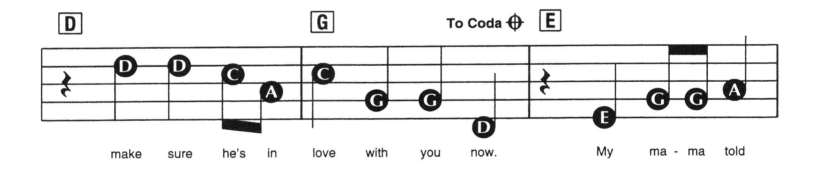

make sure he's in love with you now. My ma - ma told

D.S. al Coda
(Return to %
Play to ⊕ and
Skip to Coda)

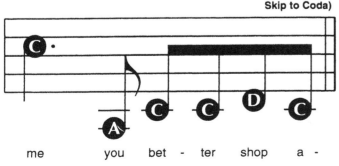

me you bet - ter shop a -

CODA
⊕

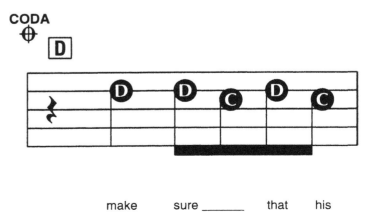

make sure _____ that his

Someday We'll Be Together

Registration 2
Rhythm: Rock or 8 - Beat

Words and Music by Jackey Beavers,
Johnny Bristol and Harvey Fuqua

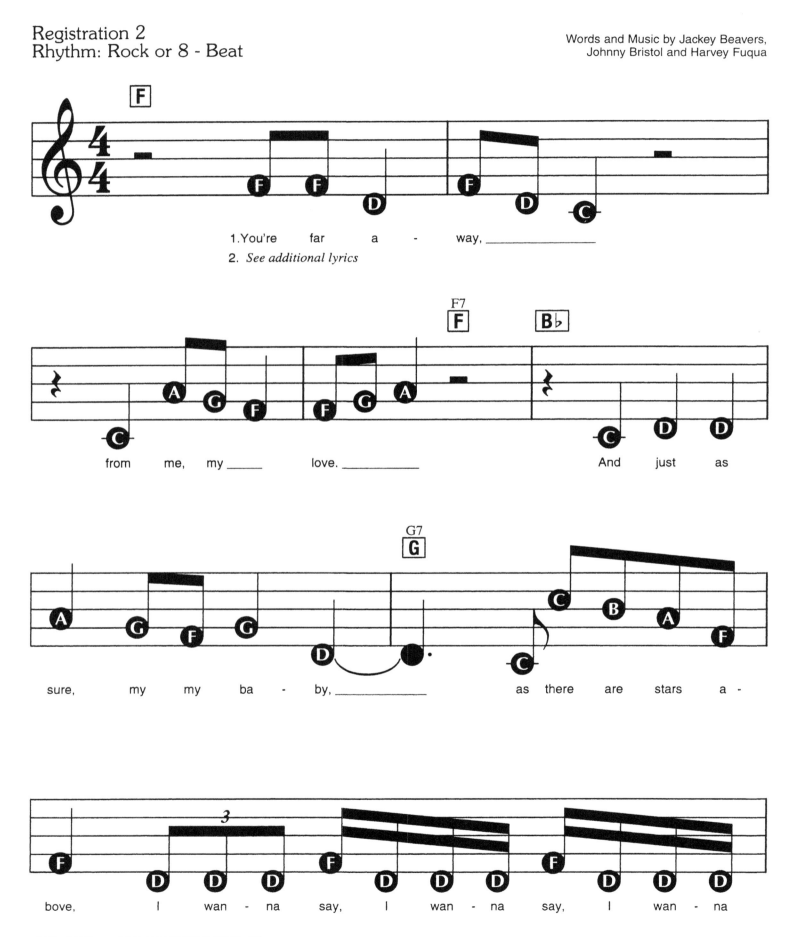

1. You're far a - way, from me, my _____ love. _____ And just as sure, my my ba - by, _____ as there are stars a - bove, I wan - na say, I wan - na say, I wan - na

2. *See additional lyrics*

105

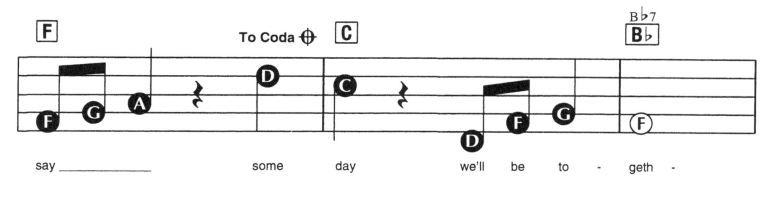

say _____ some day we'll be to - geth -

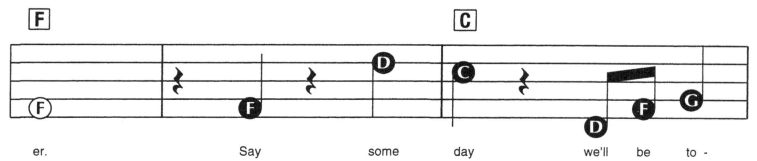

er. Say some day we'll be to -

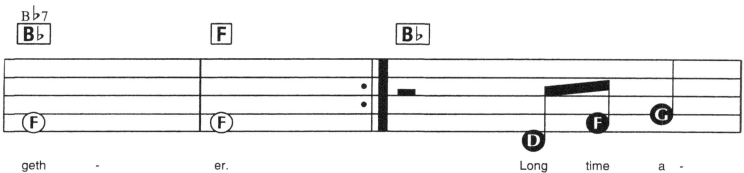

geth - er. Long time a -

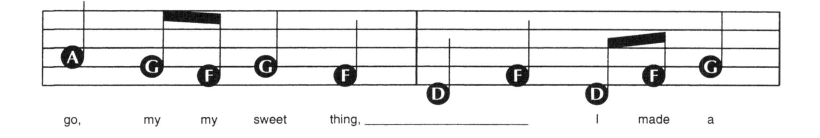

go, my my sweet thing, _____ I made a

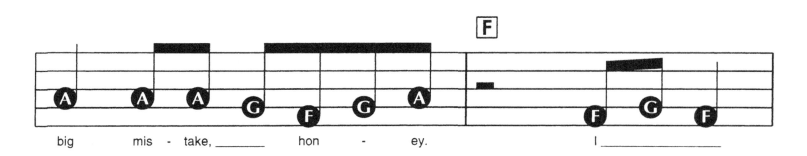

big mis - take, _____ hon - ey. I _____

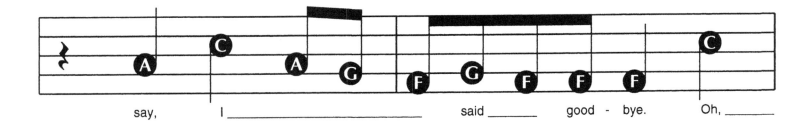

say, I _____ said _____ good - bye. Oh, _____

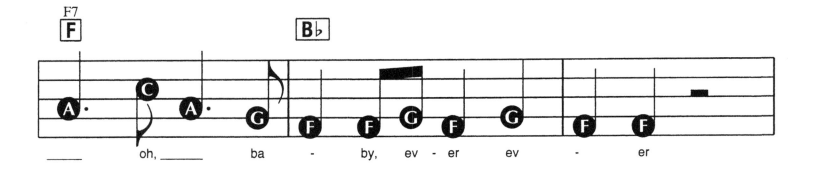

_____ oh, _____ ba - by, ev - er ev - er

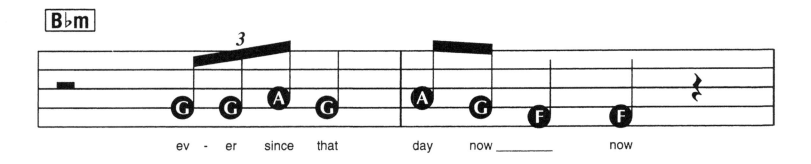

ev - er since that day now _____ now

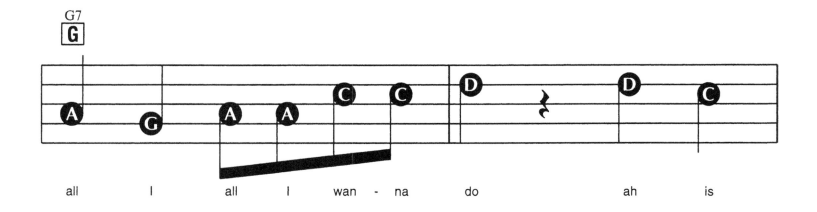

all I all I wan - na do ah is

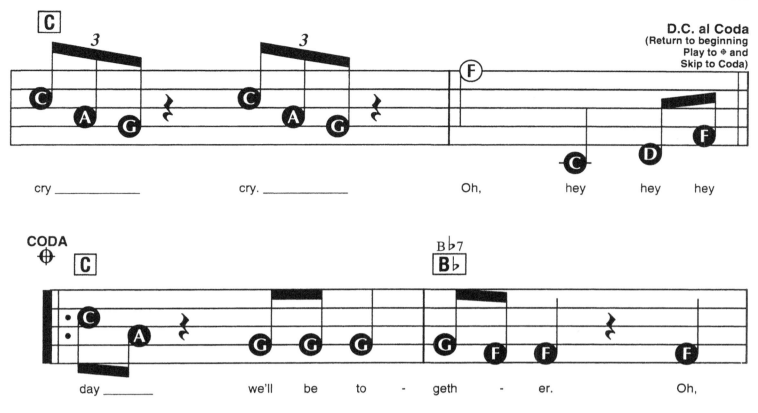

D.C. al Coda
(Return to beginning
Play to ⊕ and
Skip to Coda)

cry _____   cry. _____   Oh,   hey   hey   hey

CODA

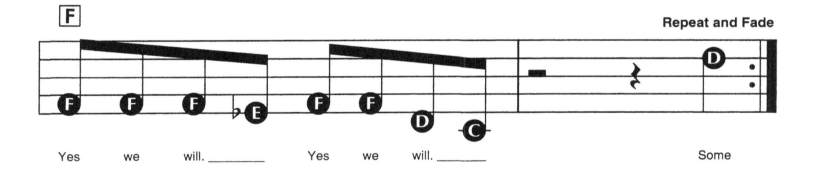

day _____   we'll   be   to - geth - er.   Oh,

Repeat and Fade

Yes   we   will. _____   Yes   we   will. _____   Some

Additional Lyrics

2. You know my love is yours, baby,
   oh, right from the start
   You, you, you posess my soul now, honey.
   And I know, I know you own my heart.
   And I wanna say someday we'll be together.
   Yes we will, yes we will.
   I long for you, every night,
   just to kiss your sweet, sweet lips,
   Hold you ever so tight and I wanna say
   Someday we'll be together.
   Oh, yes we will, yes we will.

Standing in the Shadows of Love

Registration 4
Rhythm: Rock or 8 Beat

Words and Music by Edward Holland,
Lamont Dozier and Brian Holland

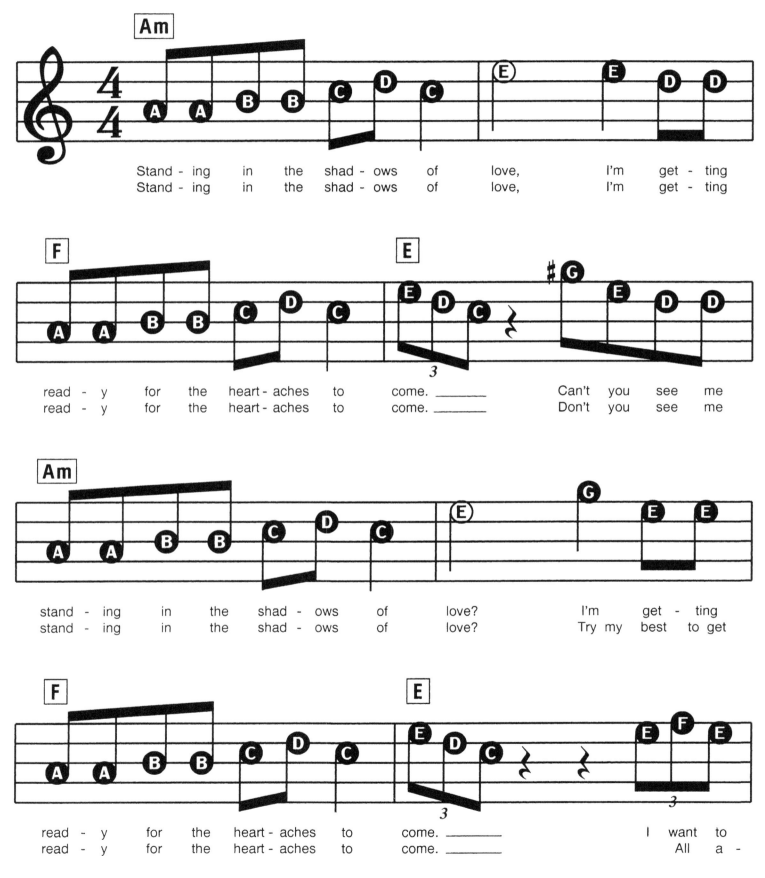

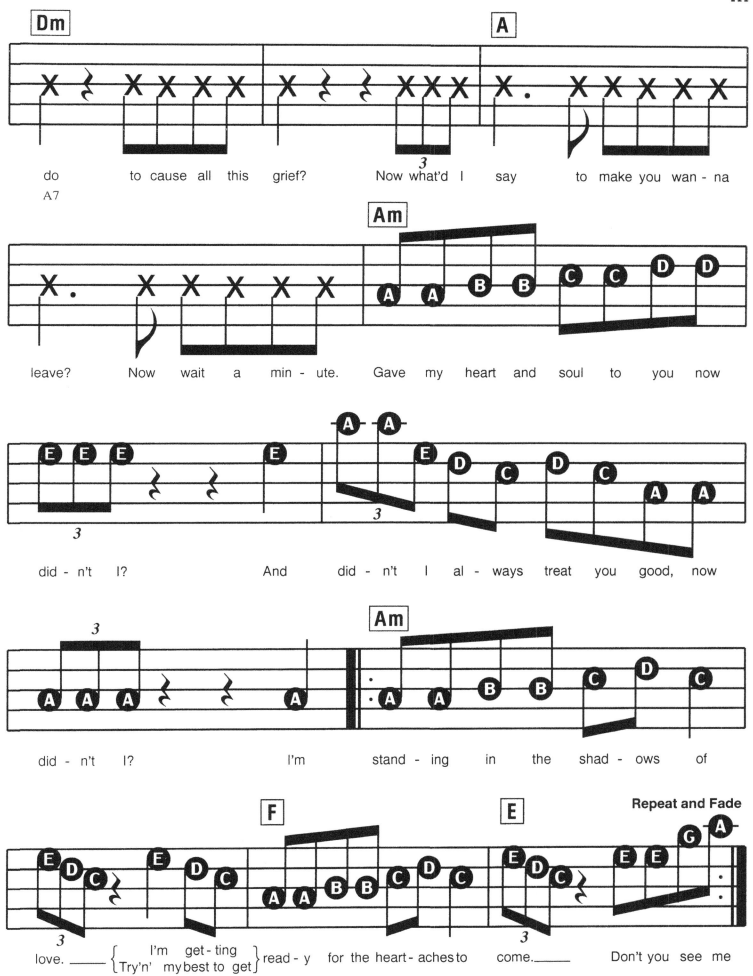

Stop! In the Name of Love

Registration 8
Rhythm: Rock or Pops

Words and Music by Lamont Dozier,
Brian Holland and Edward Holland

114

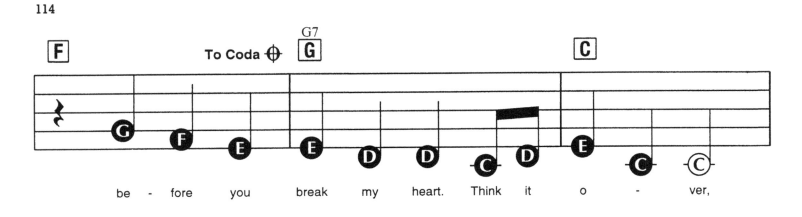

be - fore you break my heart. Think it o - ver,

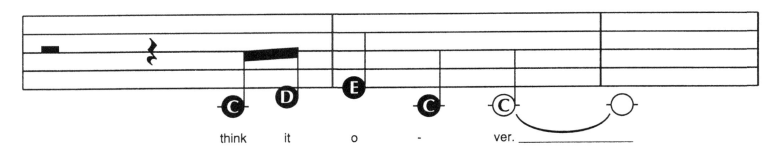

think it o - ver. _____

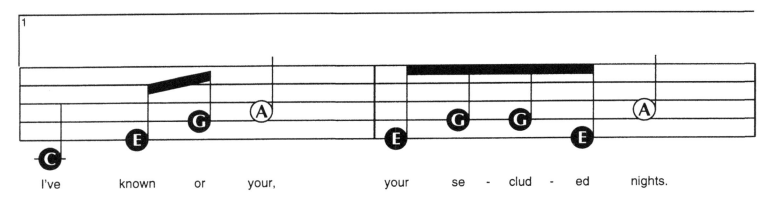

I've known or your, your se - clud - ed nights.

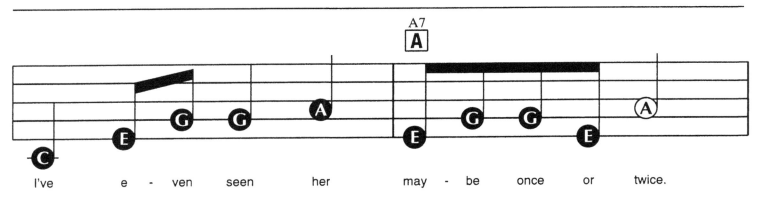

I've e - ven seen her may - be once or twice.

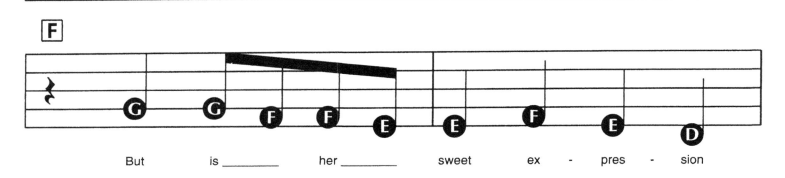

But is _____ her _____ sweet ex - pres - sion

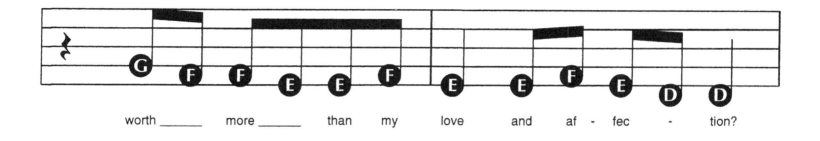

worth _____ more _____ than my love and af - fec - tion?

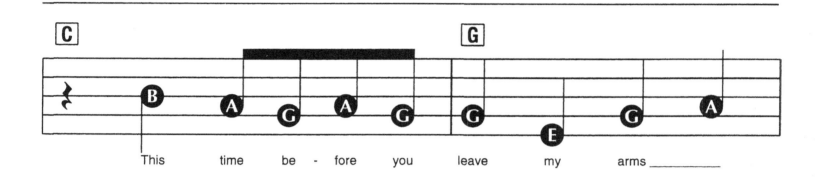

This time be - fore you leave my arms _____

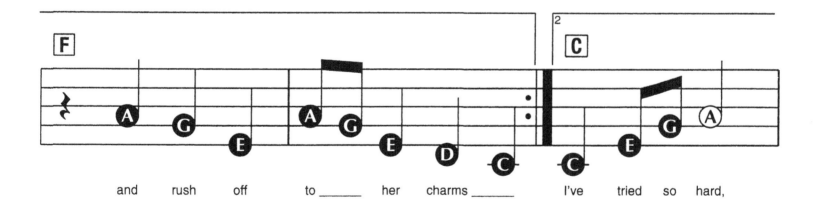

and rush off to _____ her charms _____ I've tried so hard,

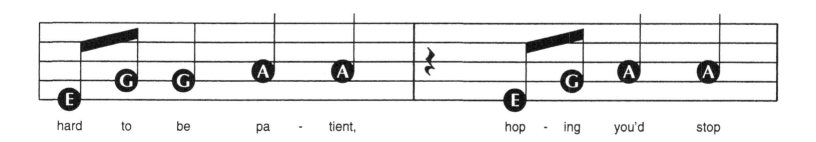

hard to be pa - tient, hop - ing you'd stop

116

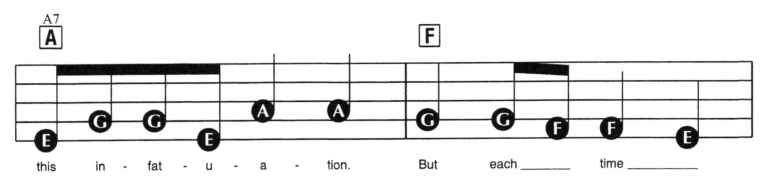

this in - fat - u - a - tion. But each _____ time _____

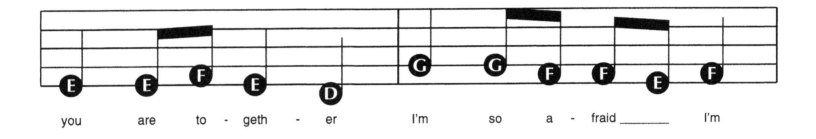

you are to - geth - er I'm so a - fraid _____ I'm

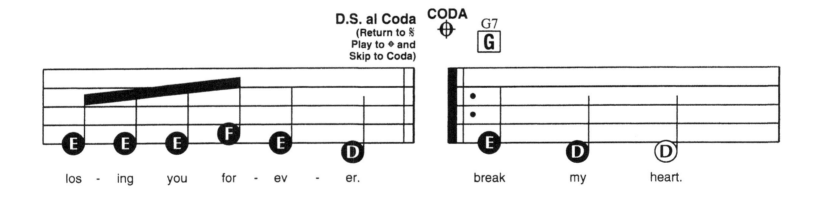

D.S. al Coda
(Return to 𝄋
Play to ⊕ and
Skip to Coda)

CODA
⊕

los - ing you for - ev - er. break my heart.

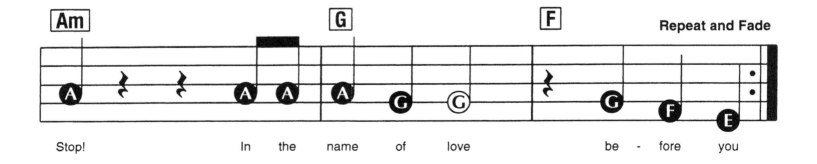

Repeat and Fade

Stop! In the name of love be - fore you

Three Times a Lady

Registration 1
Rhythm: Waltz

Words and Music by
Lionel Richie

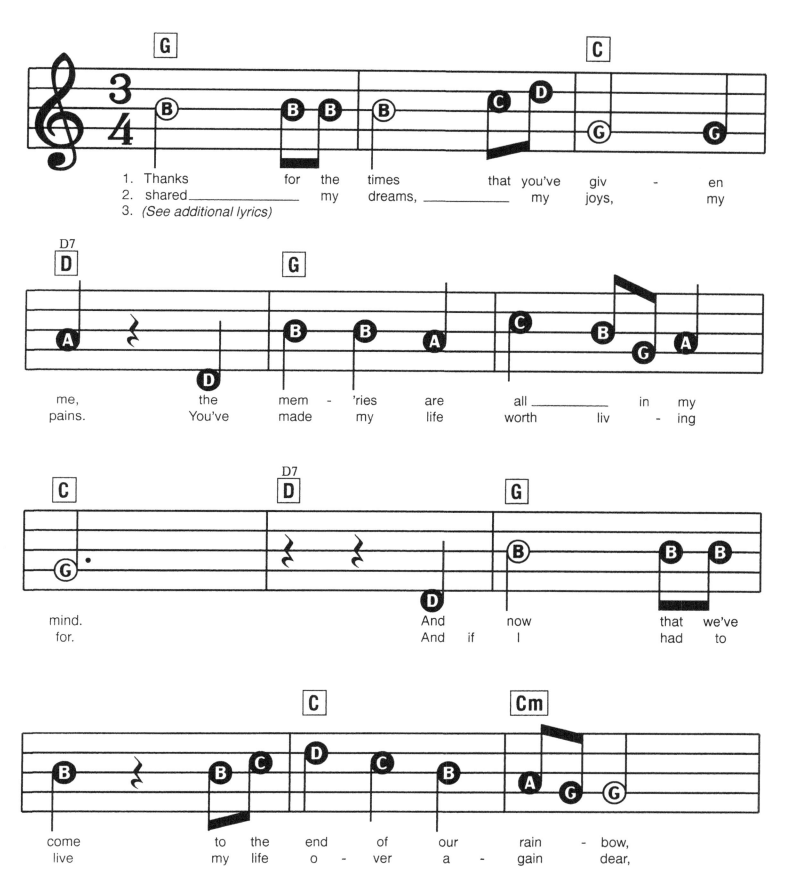

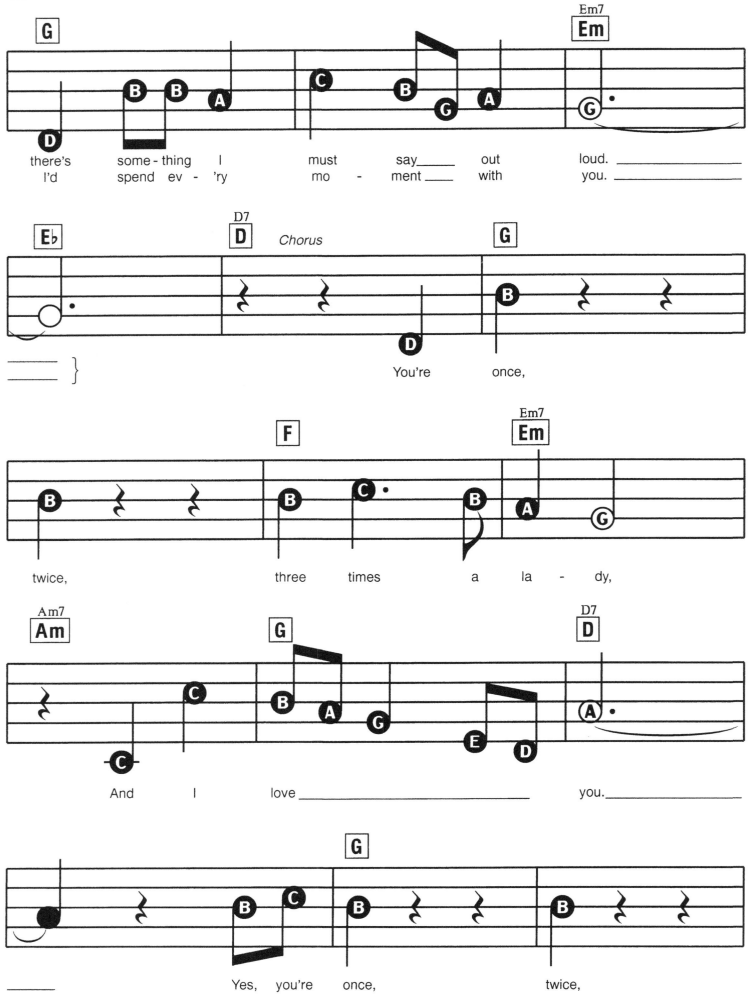

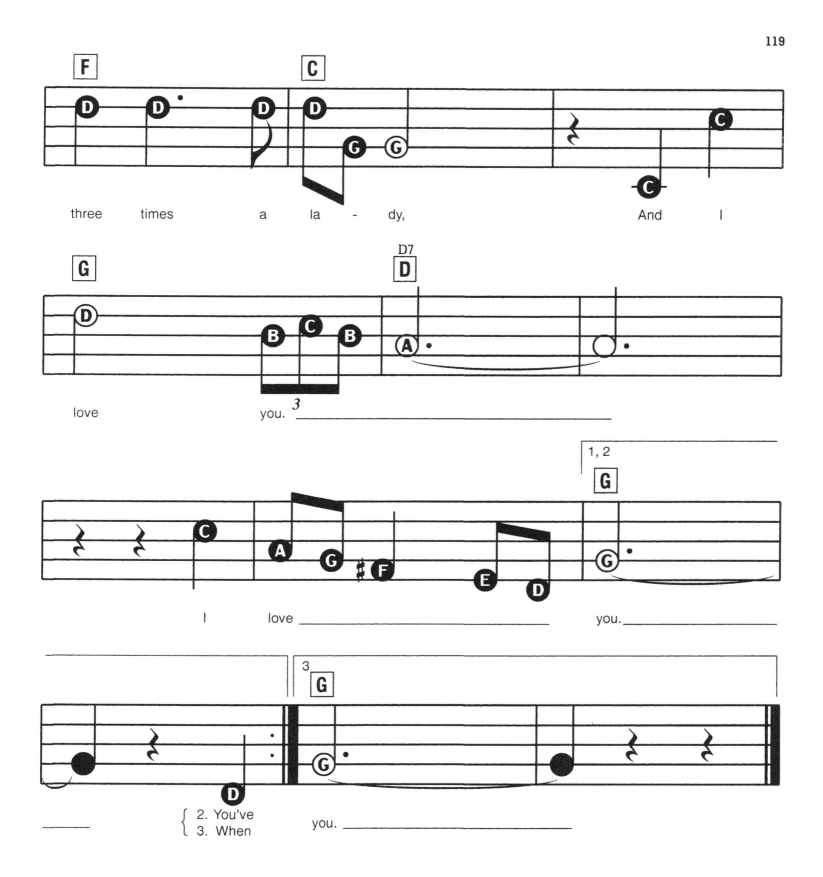

three times a la - dy, And I

love you. *3*

I love you.

{ 2. You've
{ 3. When you.

Additional Lyrics

3. When we are together the moments I cherish
   With ev'ry beat of my heart.
   To touch you, to hold you, to feel you, to need you.
   There's nothing to keep us apart.
   Chorus

Touch Me in the Morning

Registration 1
Rhythm: Rock or 8 Beat

Words and Music by Ronald Miller
and Michael Masser

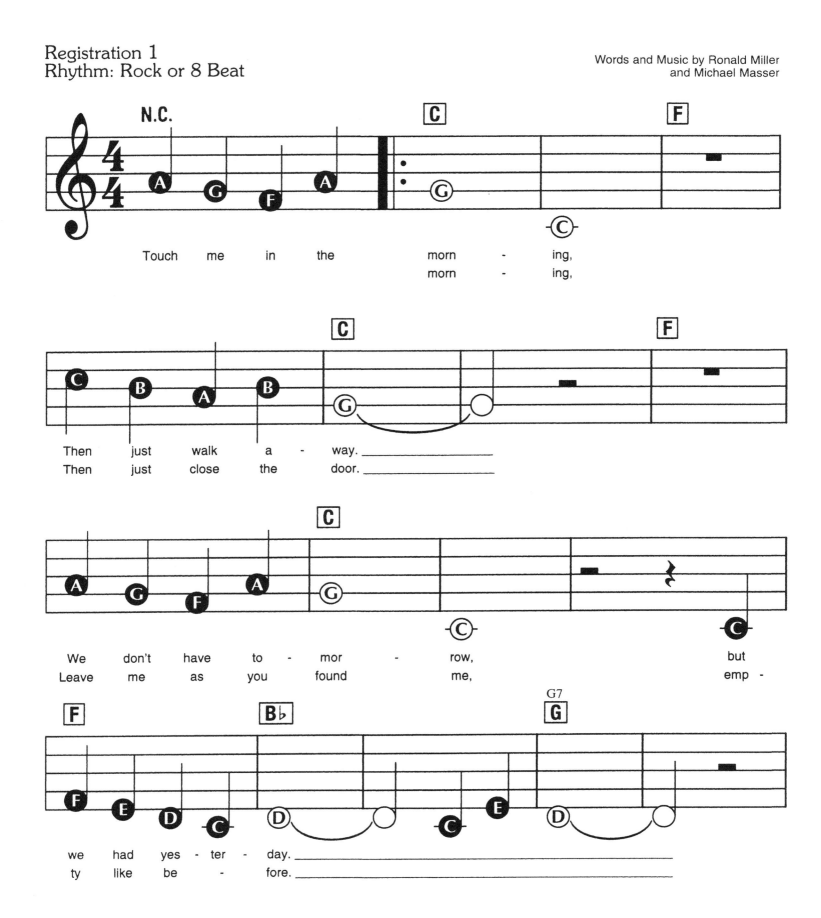

121

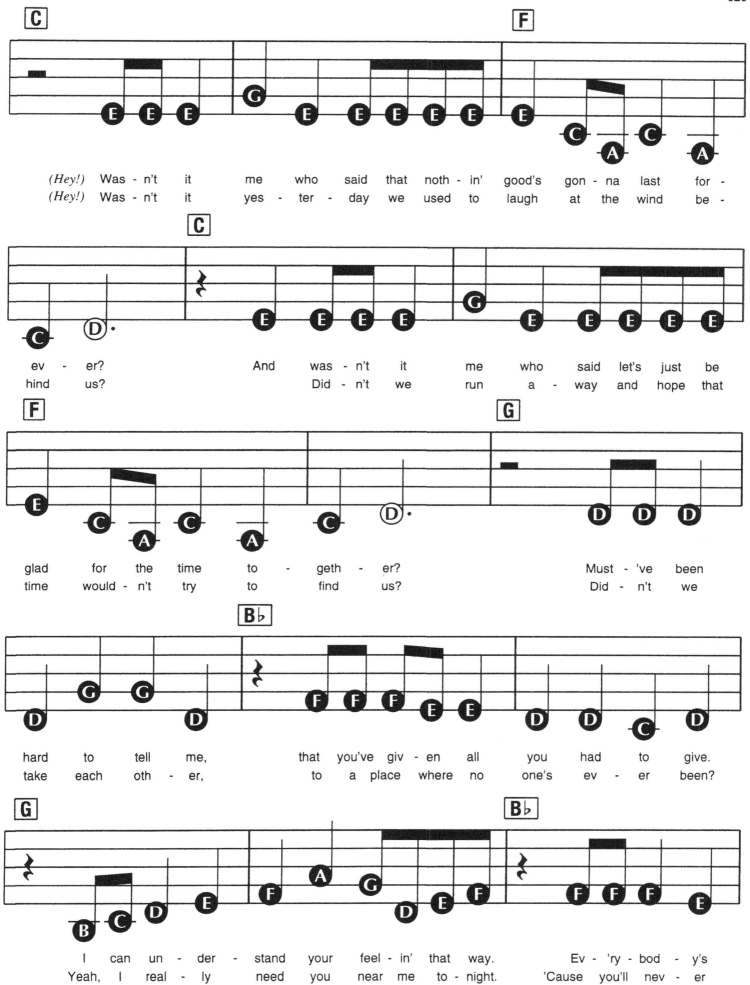

122

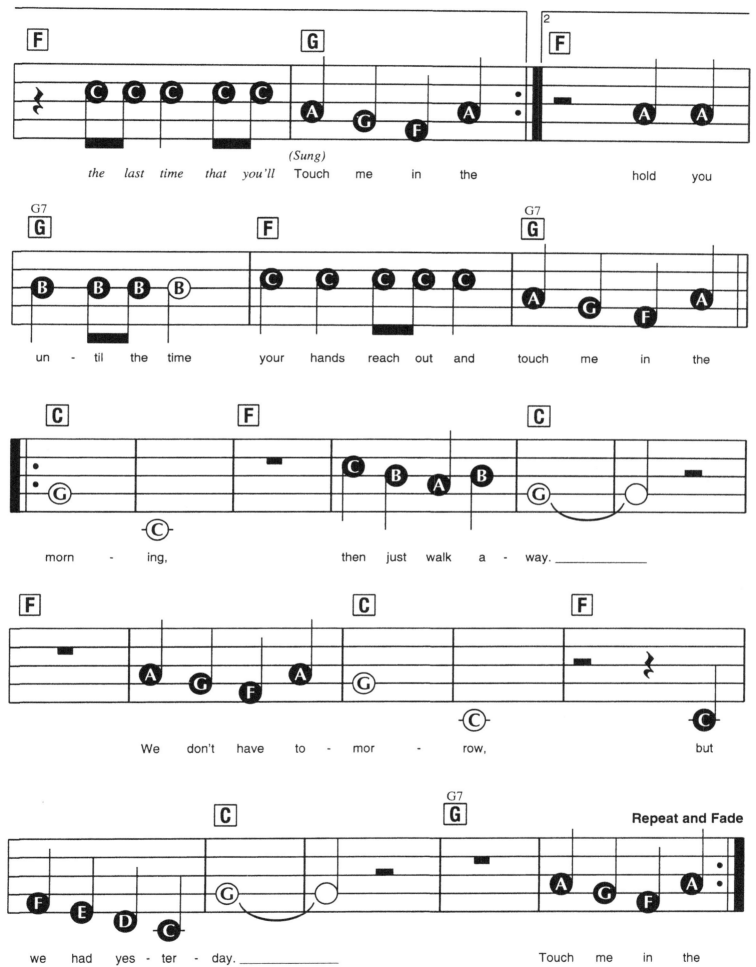

The Tracks of My Tears

Registration 2
Rhythm: Rock or 8 Beat

Words and Music by William "Smokey" Robinson,
Warren Moore and Marvin Tarplin

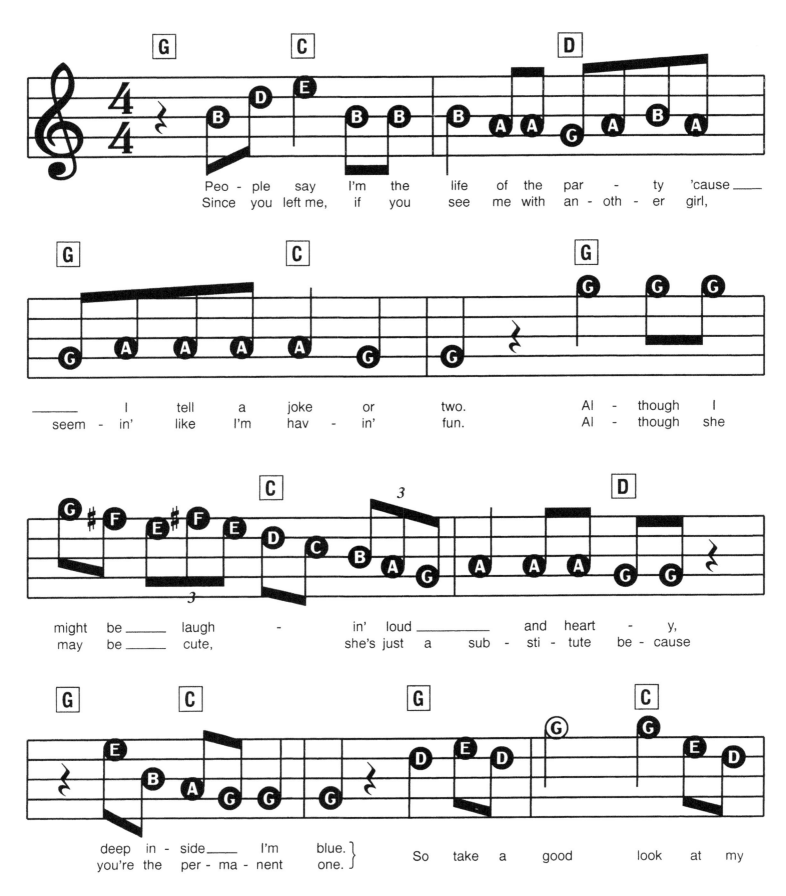

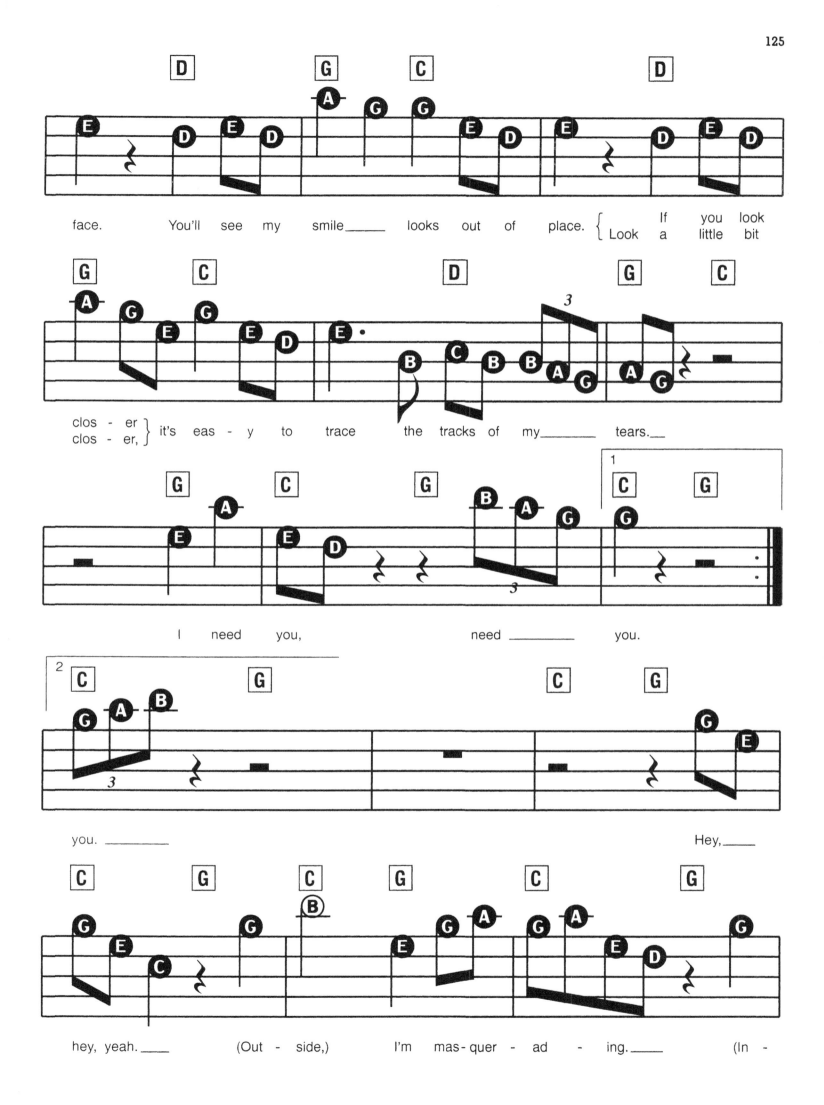

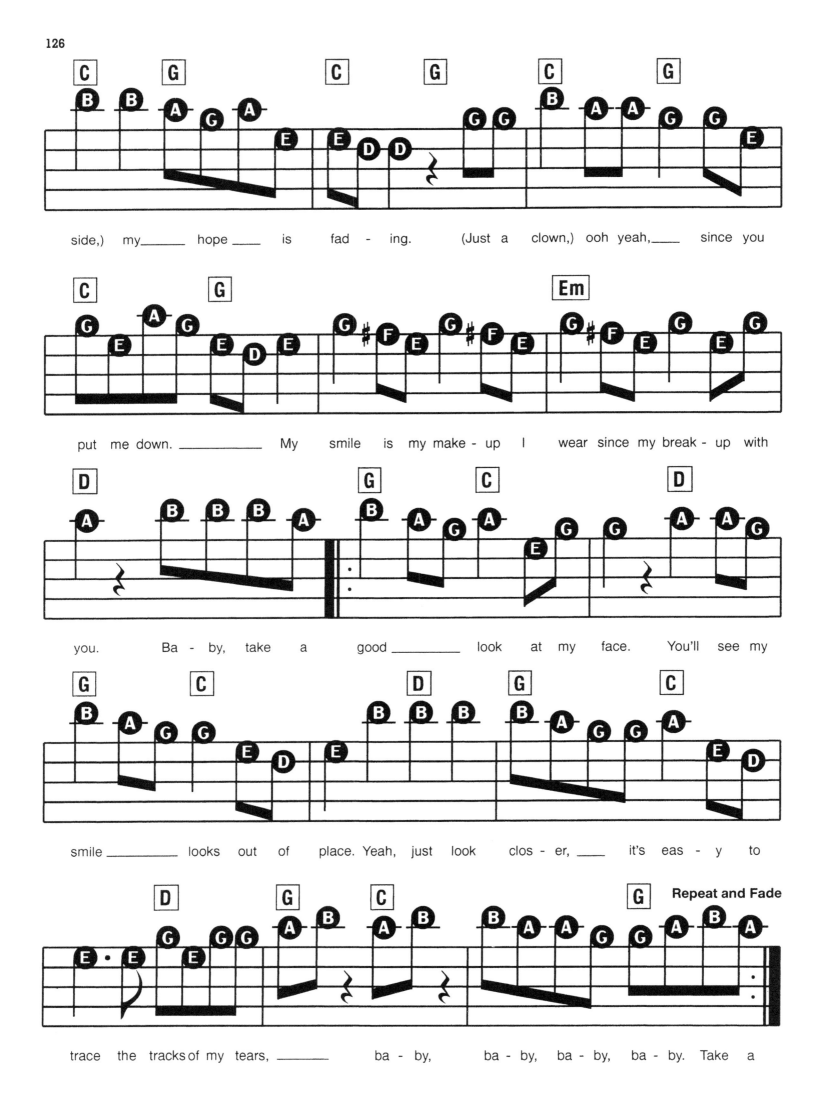

The Way You Do the Things You Do

Registration 7
Rhythm: Shuffle or Reggae

Words and Music by William "Smokey" Robinson
and Robert Rogers

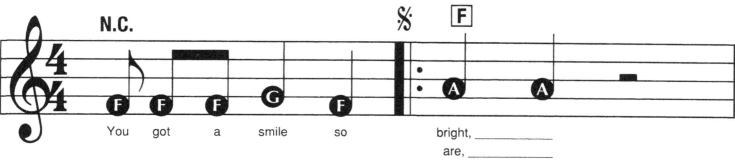

You got a smile so bright, _____
are, _____

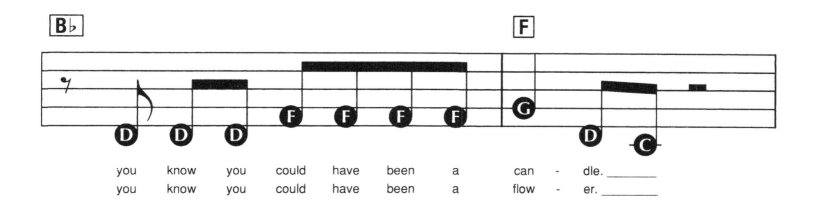

you know you could have been a can - dle. _____
you know you could have been a flow - er. _____

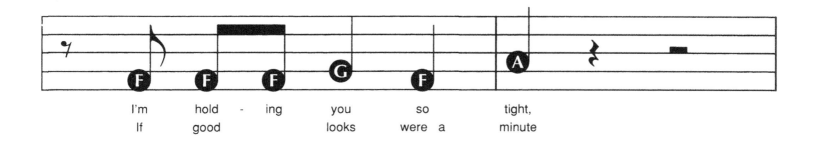

I'm hold - ing you so tight,
If good looks were a minute

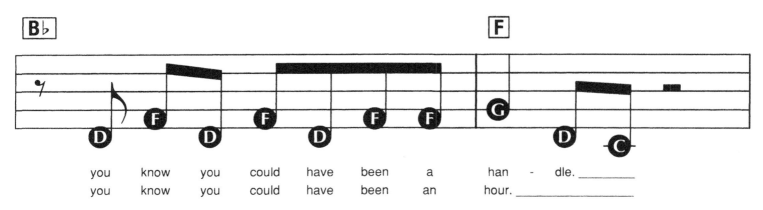

you know you could have been a han - dle. _____
you know you could have been an hour. _____

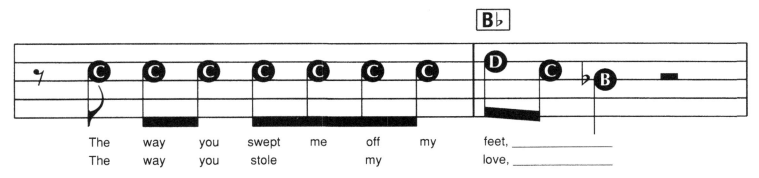

The way you swept me off my feet, _____
The way you stole my love, _____

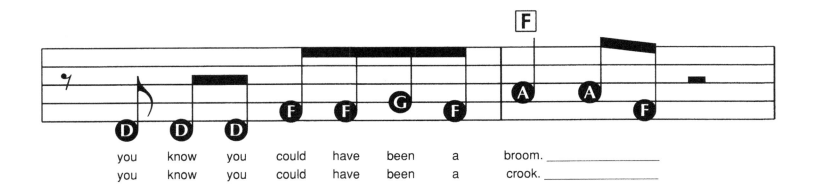

you know you could have been a broom. _____
you know you could have been a crook. _____

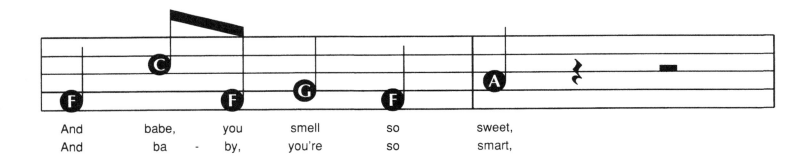

And babe, you smell so sweet,
And ba - by, you're so smart,

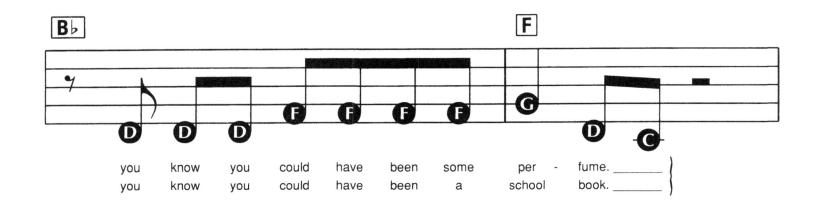

you know you could have been some per - fume. _____ }
you know you could have been a school book. _____ }

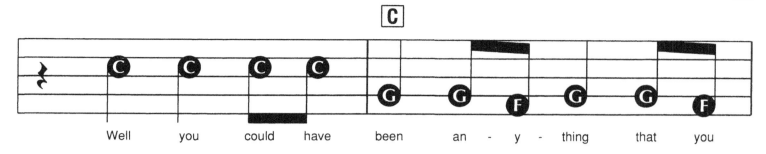

Well you could have been an - y - thing that you

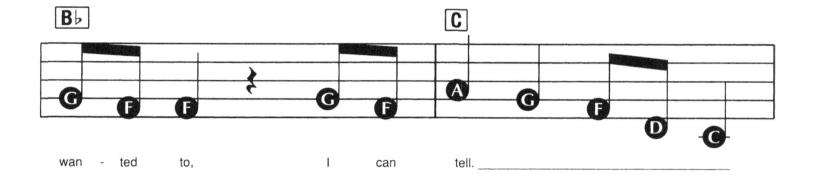

wan - ted to, I can tell. _____

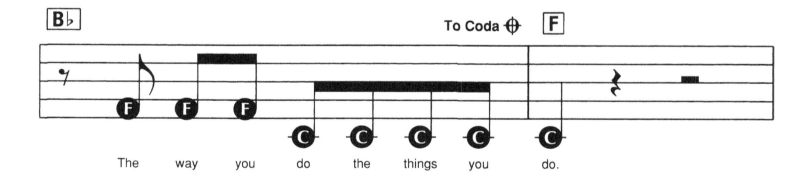

To Coda ⊕

The way you do the things you do.

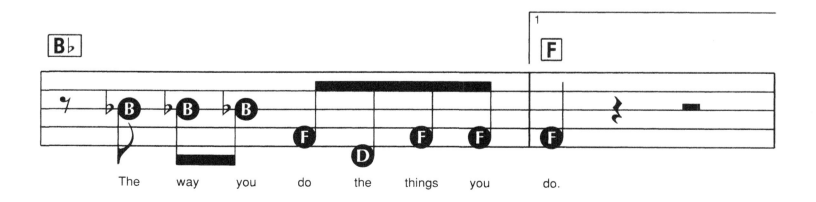

The way you do the things you do.

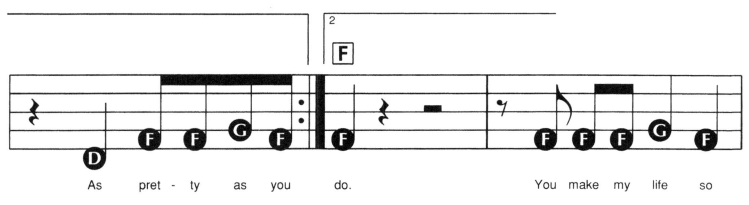

As pret - ty as you do.   You make my life so

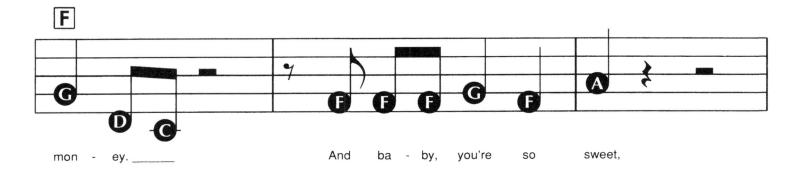

rich,   you know you could have been some

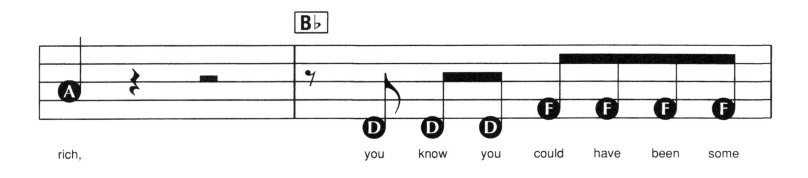

mon - ey. _____   And ba - by, you're so sweet,

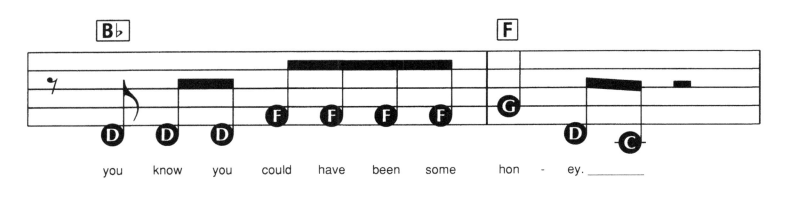

you know you could have been some hon - ey. _____

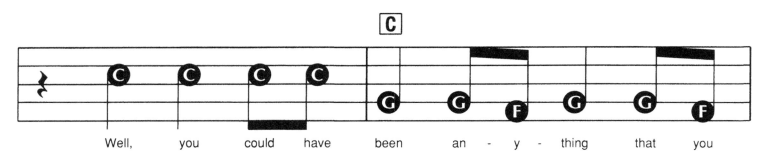

Well, you could have been an - y - thing that you

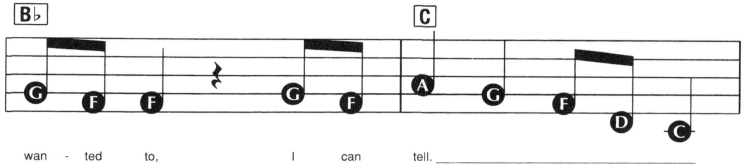

wan - ted to, I can tell. _____

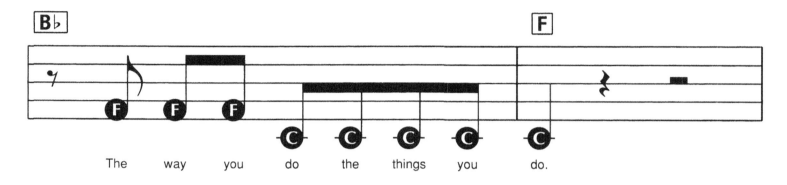

The way you do the things you do.

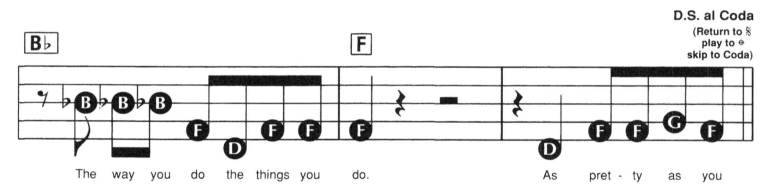

The way you do the things you do. As pret - ty as you

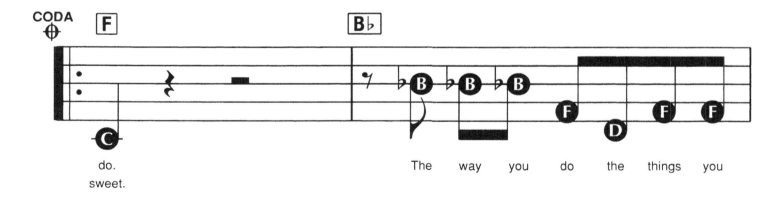

do.
sweet.

The way you do the things you

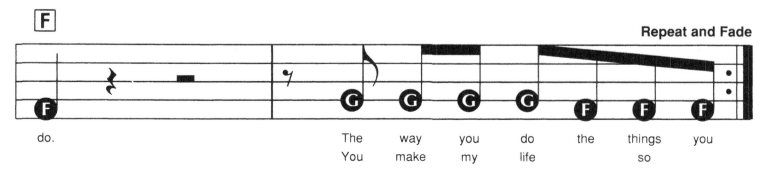

do.

The way you do the things you
You make my life so

What's Going On

Registration 7
Rhythm: Rock or 16 - Beat

Words and Music by Marvin Gaye,
Al Cleveland and Renaldo Benson

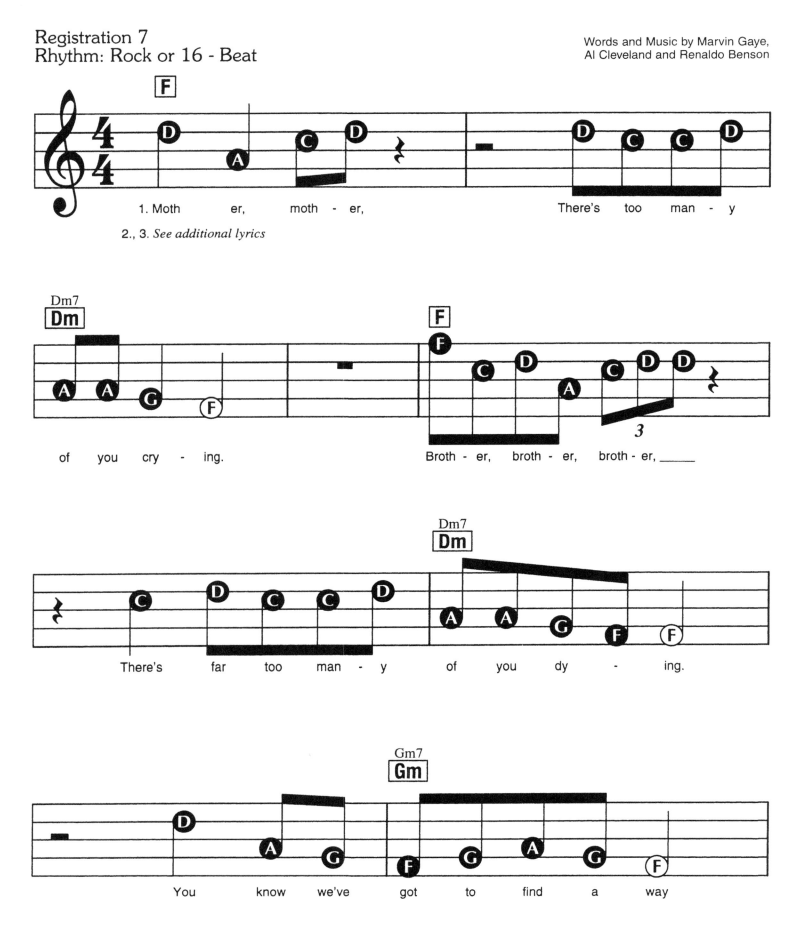

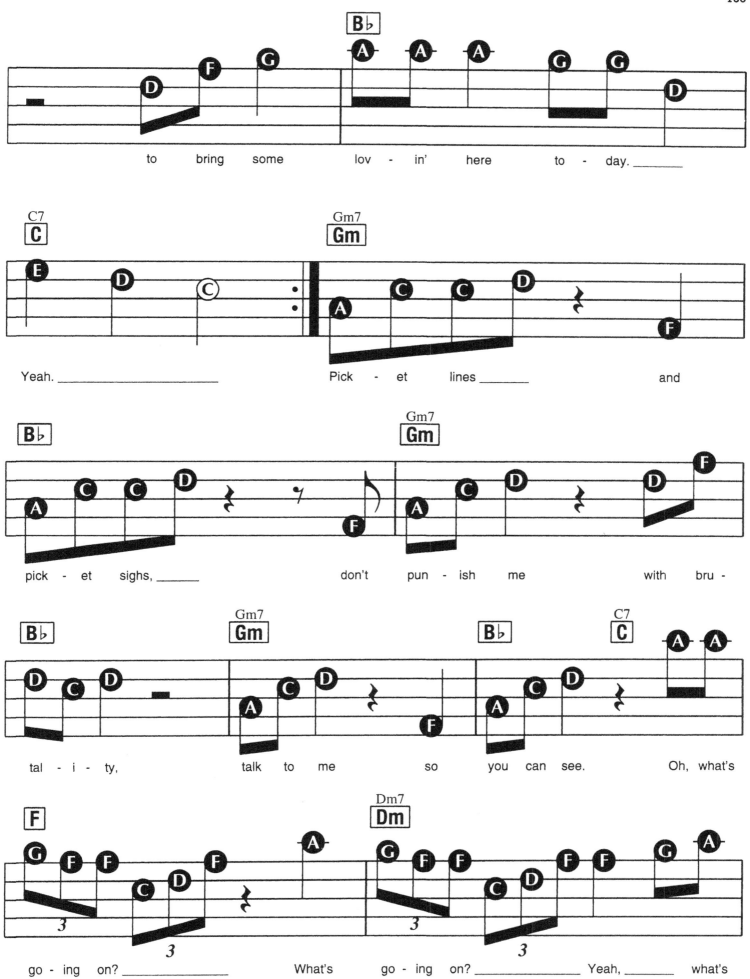

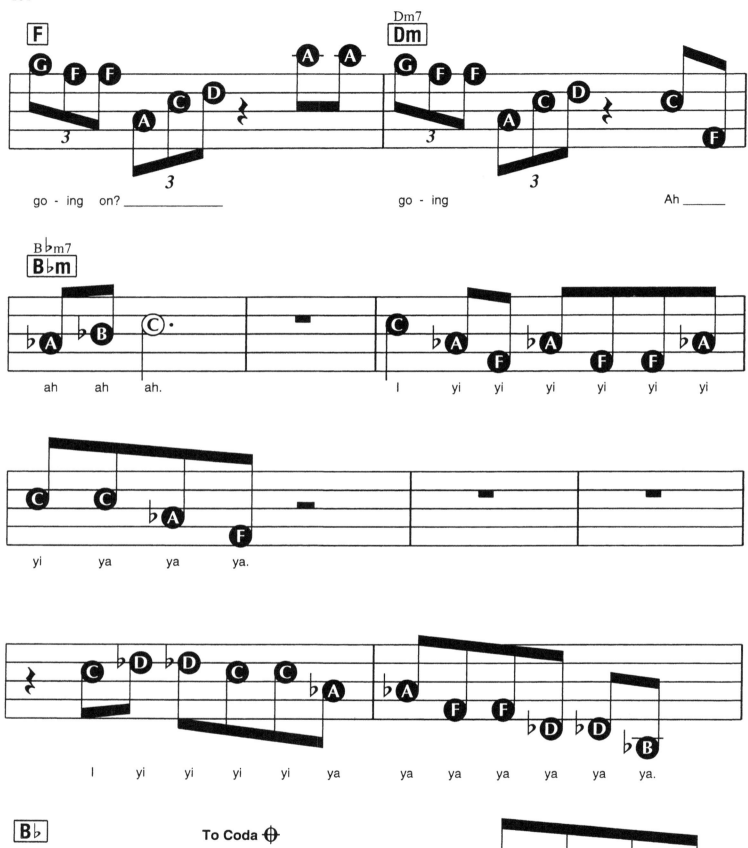

go - ing on? _____

go - ing

Ah _____

ah ah ah.

I yi yi yi yi yi

yi ya ya ya.

I yi yi yi yi ya ya ya ya ya ya ya.

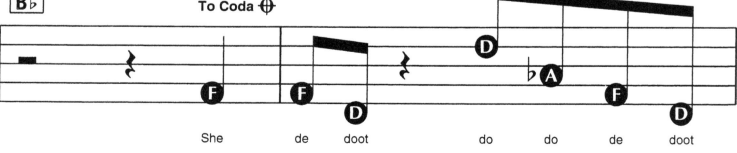

She de doot do do de doot

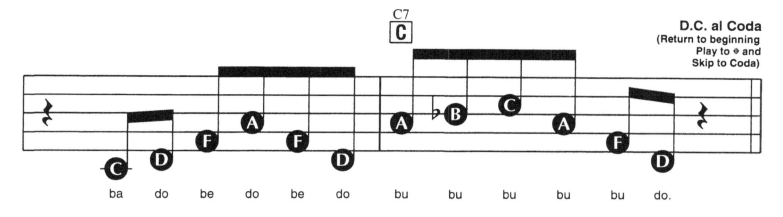

ba do be do be do bu bu bu bu bu do.

CODA

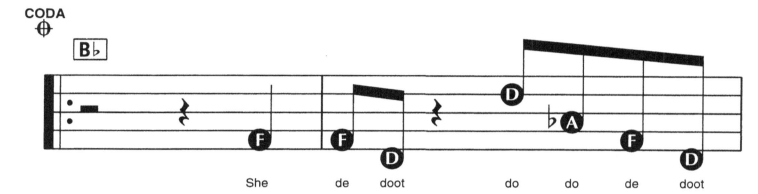

She de doot do do de doot

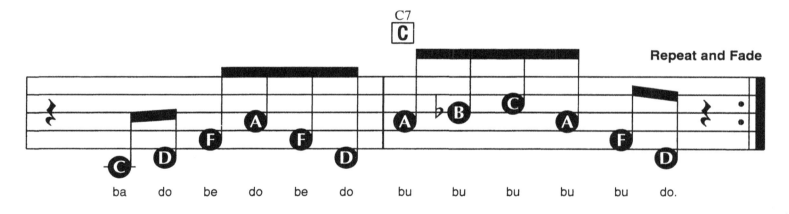

ba do be do be do bu bu bu bu bu do.

Additional Lyrics

2. Father, father, we don't need to escalate,
You see, war is not the answer, for only love can conquer hate.
You know we've got to find a way to bring some lovin' here today. *(Chorus)*

3. Father, father, everybody thinks we're wrong.
Oh but, who are they to judge us simply because our hair is long?
Oh, you know we've got to find a way bring some understanding here today. *(Chorus)*

Where Did Our Love Go

Registration 2
Rhythm: Swing or Shuffle

Words and Music by Brian Holland,
Lamont Dozier and Edward Holland

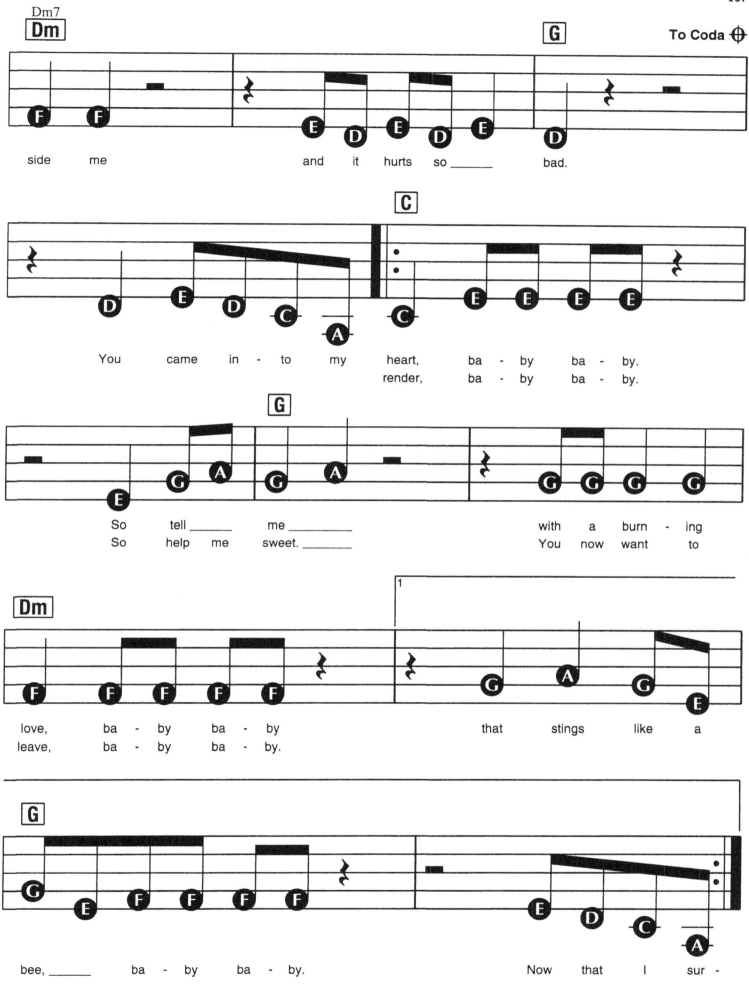

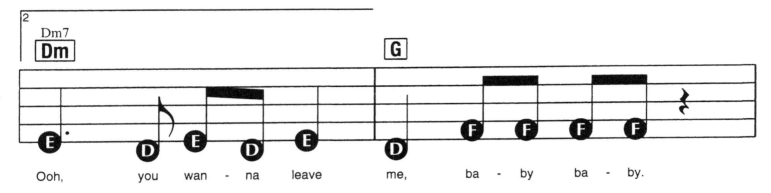

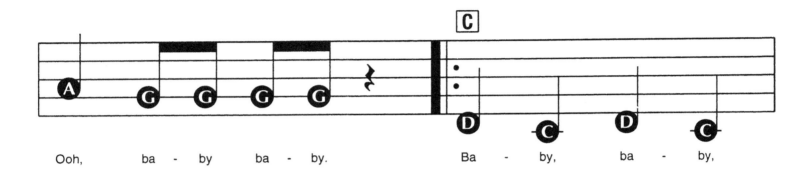

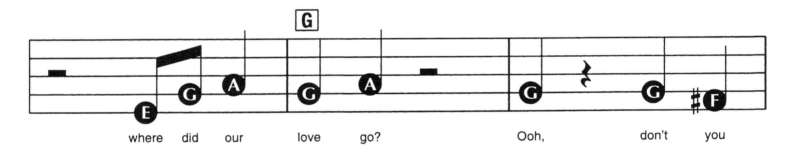

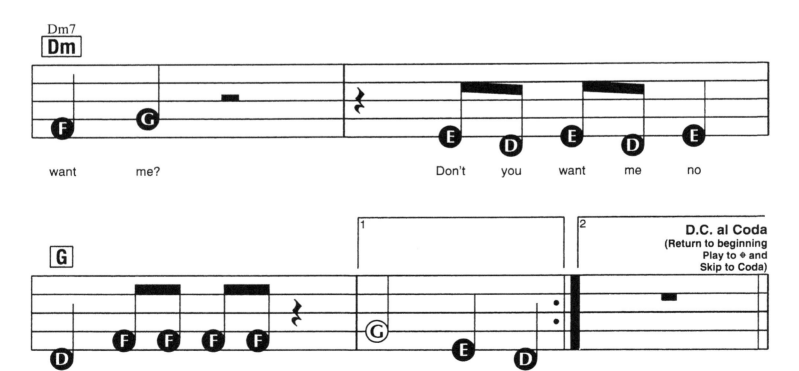

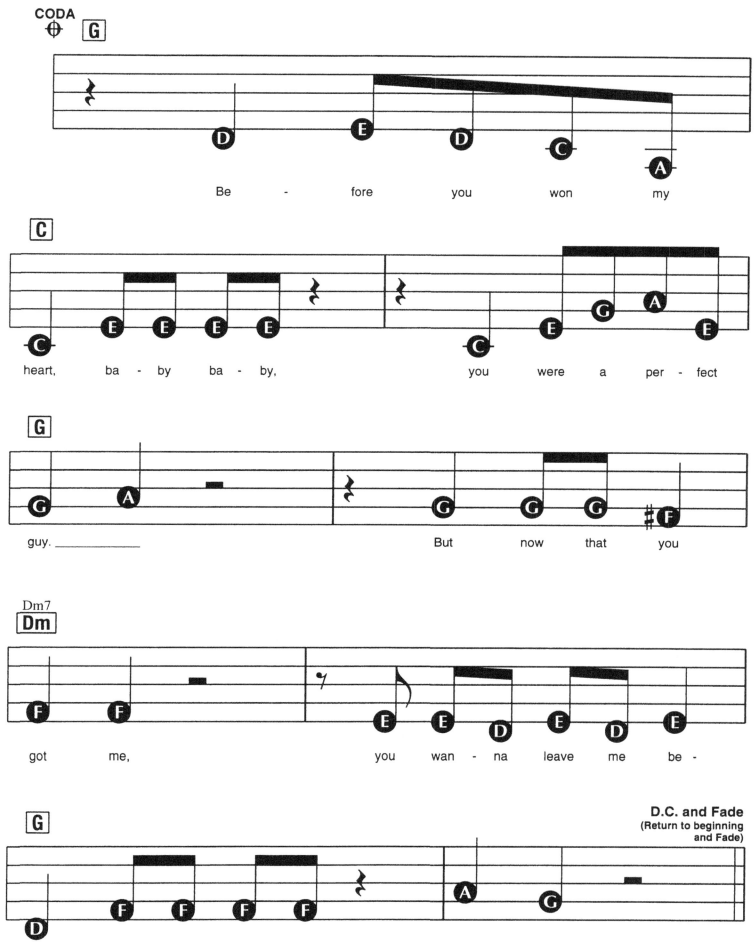

CODA

G

Be - fore you won my

C

heart, ba - by ba - by, you were a per - fect

G

guy. _____ But now that you

Dm7
Dm

got me, you wan - na leave me be -

G

D.C. and Fade
(Return to beginning
and Fade)

hind, ba - by ba - by. Ooh. _____

You Can't Hurry Love

Registration 2
Rhythm: Rock

Words and Music by Edward Holland,
Lamont Dozier and Brian Holland

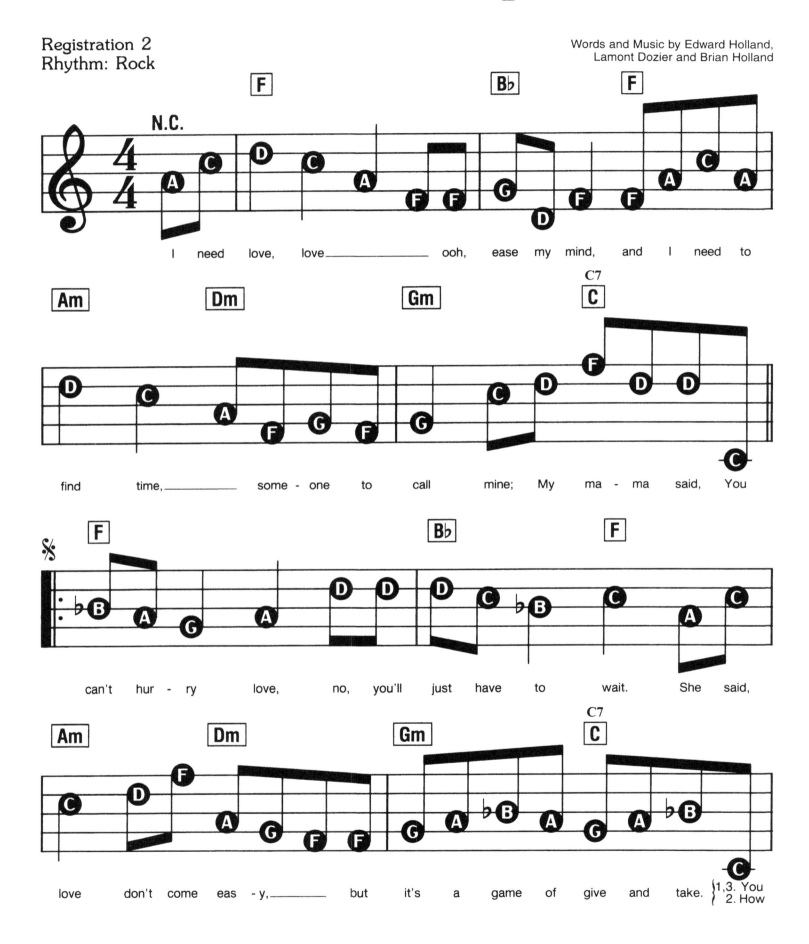

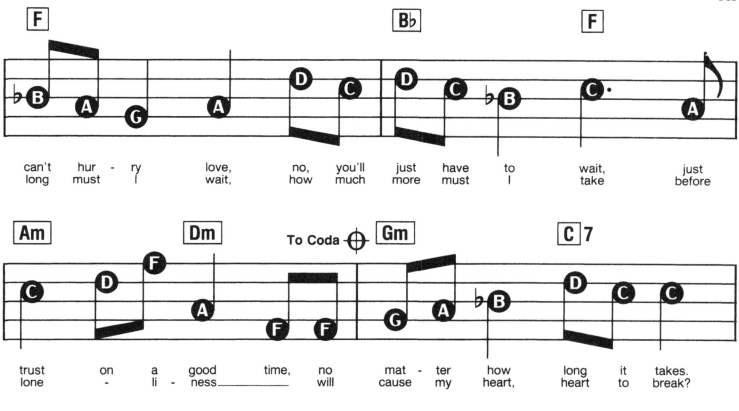

F **Bb** **F**

can't hur - ry love, no, you'll just have to wait, just
long must I wait, how much more must I take, before

Am **Dm** To Coda ⊕ **Gm** **C** 7

trust on a good time, no mat - ter how long it takes.
lone - li - ness_____ will cause my heart, heart to break?

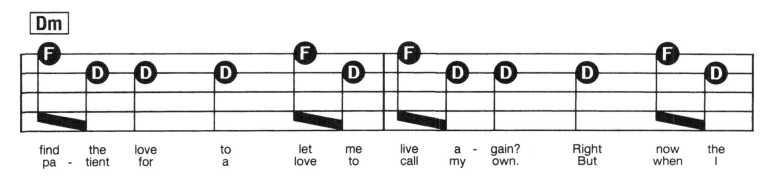

Am

How man - y heart - aches must I stand be - fore I
No, I can't bear to live my life alone. I grow im -

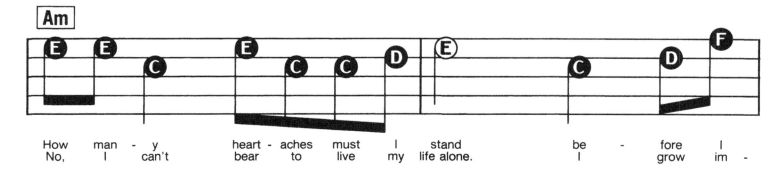

Dm

find the love to let me live a - gain? Right now the
pa - tient for a love to call my own. But when I

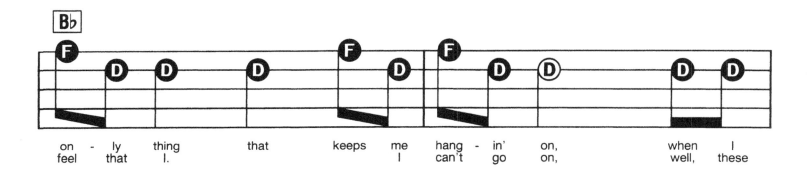

Bb

on - ly thing that keeps me hang - in' on, when I
feel that thing I. I can't go on, well, these

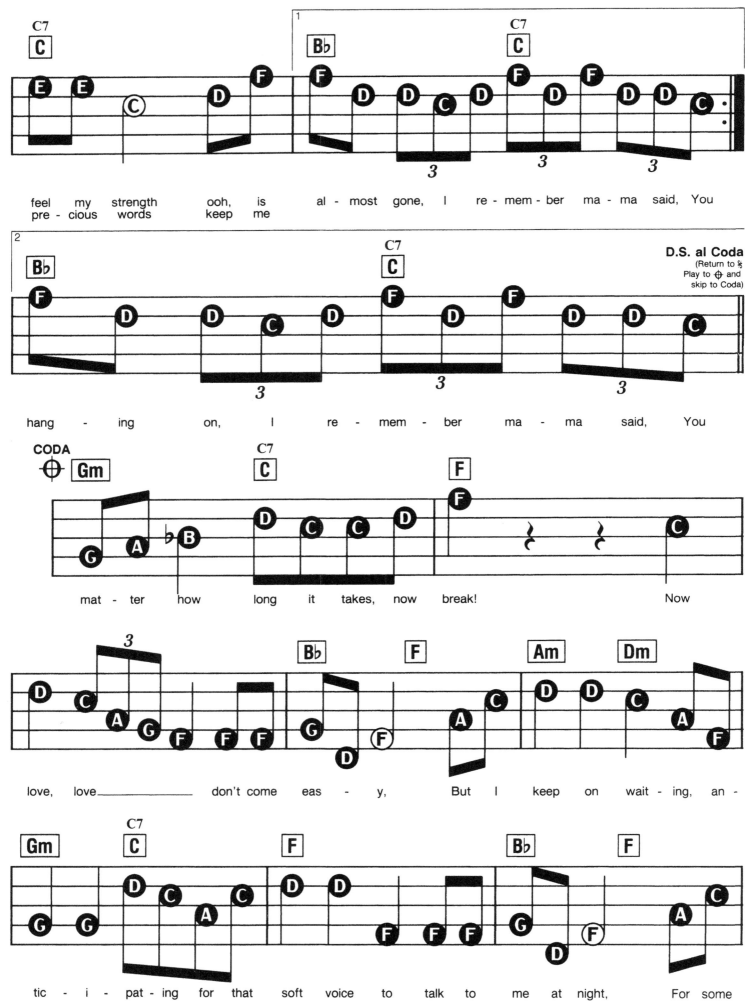

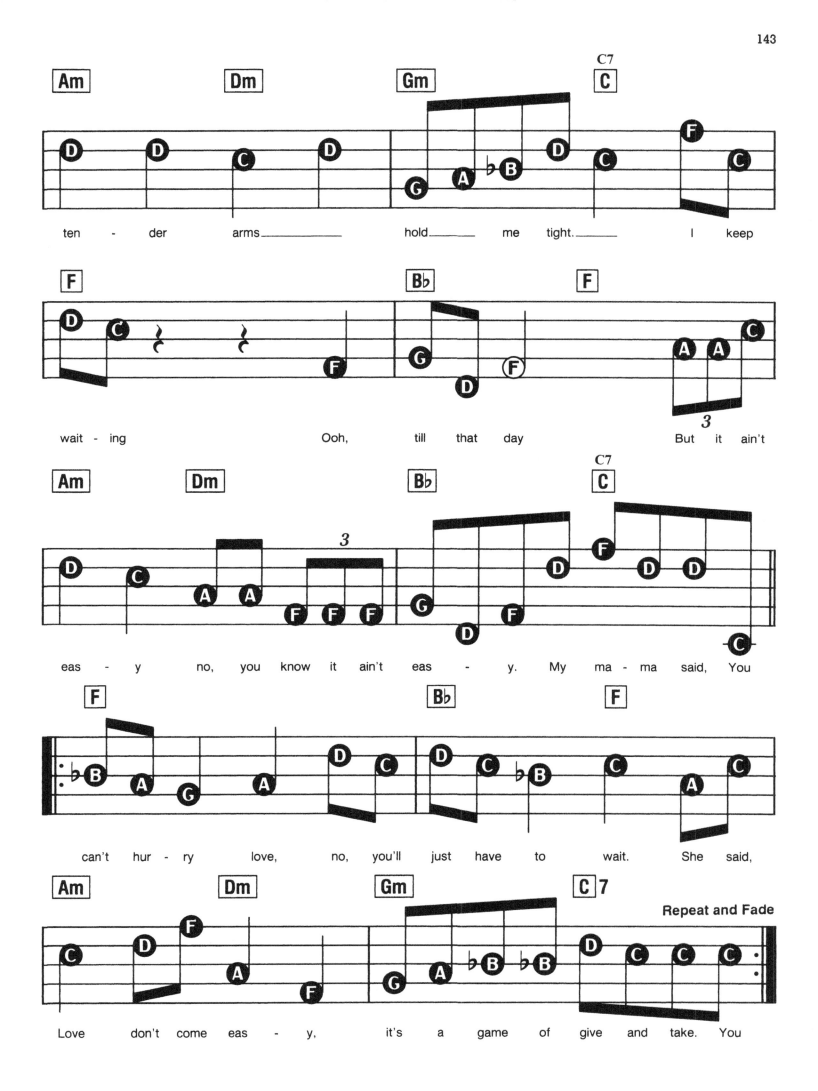

You've Really Got a Hold on Me

Registration 8
Rhythm: Slow Rock

Words and Music by
William "Smokey" Robinson

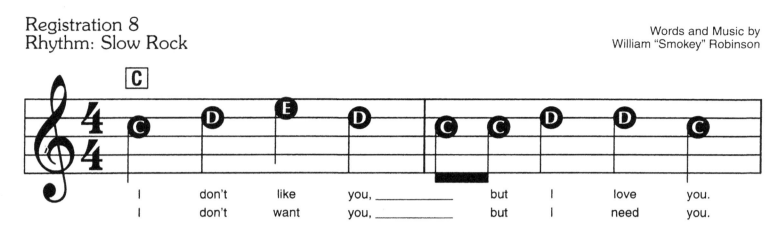

I don't like you, _____ but I love you.
I don't want you, _____ but I need you.

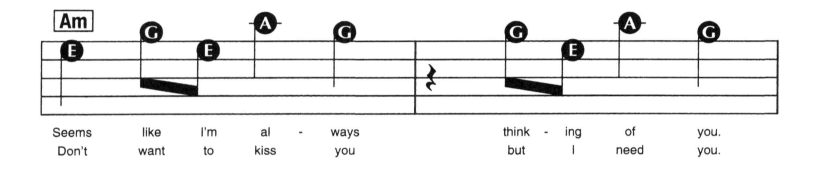

Seems like I'm al - ways think - ing of you.
Don't want to kiss you but I need you.

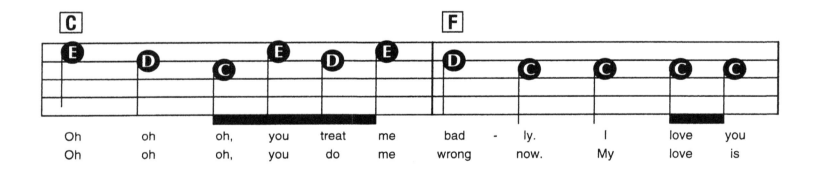

Oh oh oh, you treat me bad - ly. I love you
Oh oh oh, you do me wrong now. My love is

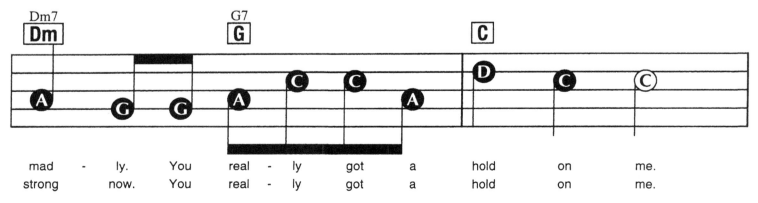

mad - ly. You real - ly got a hold on me.
strong now. You real - ly got a hold on me.

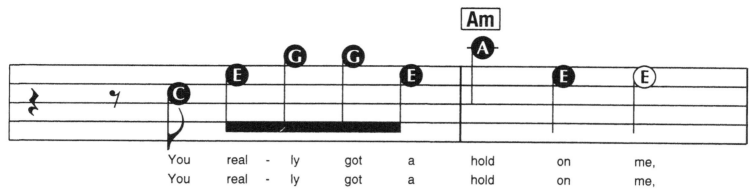

You real - ly got a hold on me,
You real - ly got a hold on me,

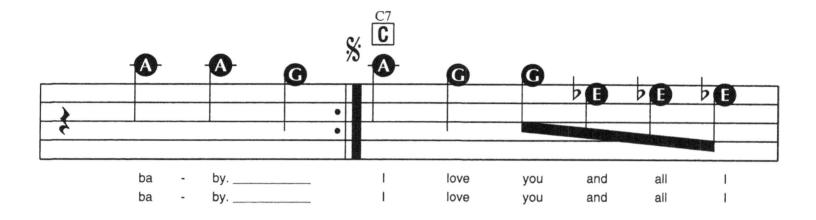

ba - by. _____ I love you and all I
ba - by. _____ I love you and all I

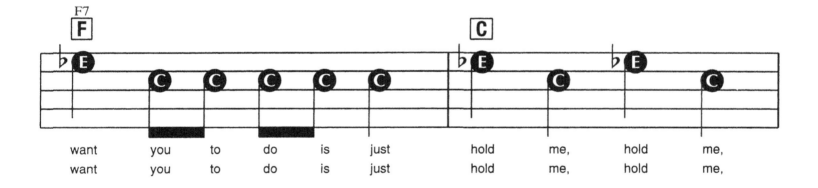

want you to do is just hold me, hold me,
want you to do is just hold me, hold me,

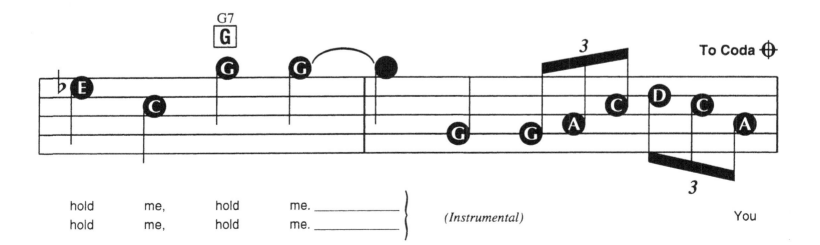

To Coda

hold me, hold me. _____ *(Instrumental)* You
hold me, hold me. _____

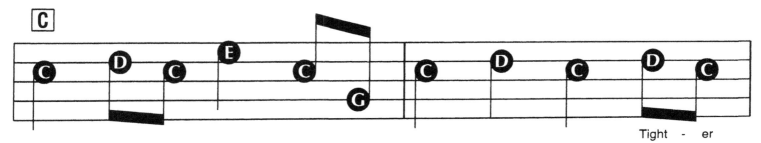

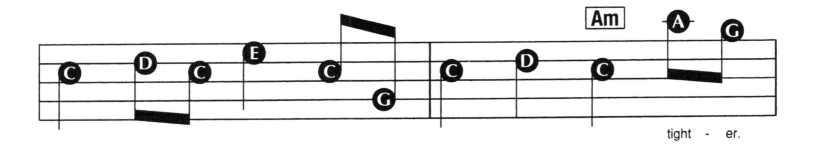

Tight - er

tight - er.

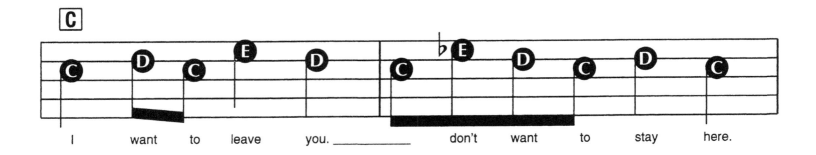

I   want   to   leave   you. _____   don't   want   to   stay   here.

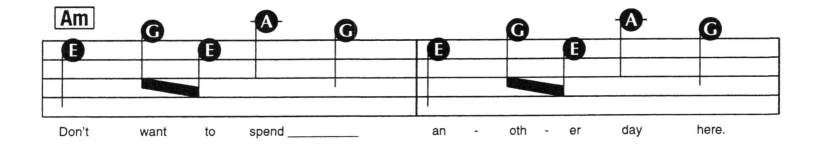

Don't   want   to   spend _____   an - oth - er   day   here.

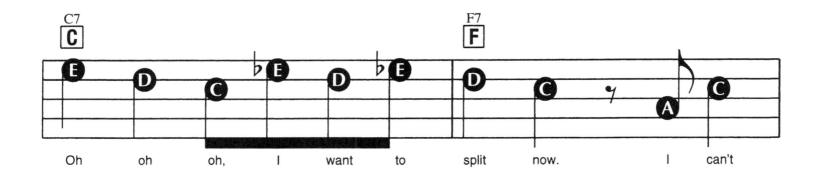

Oh   oh   oh,   I   want   to   split   now.   I   can't

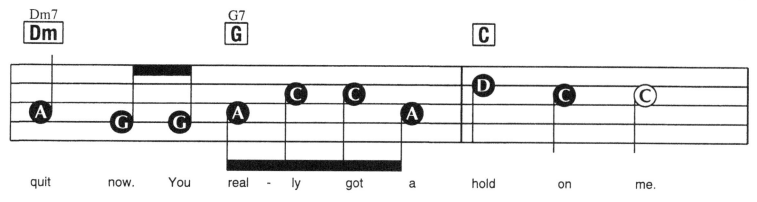

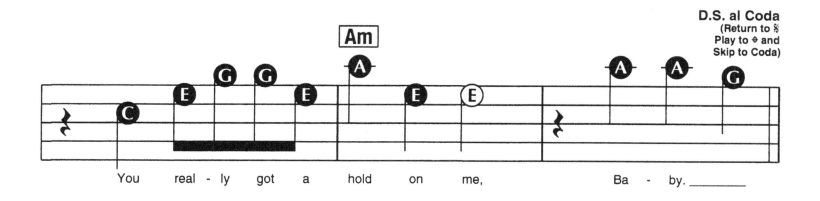

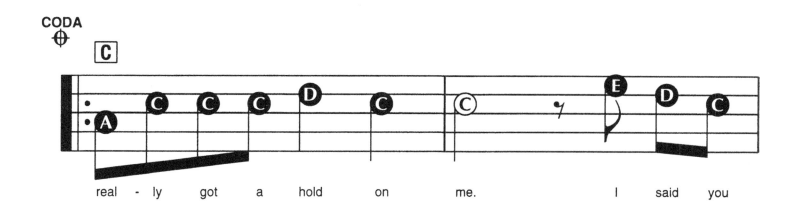

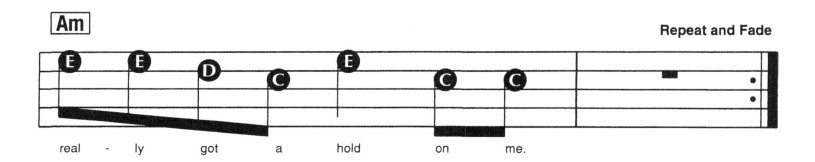

You Keep Me Hangin' On

Registration 5
Rhythm: Rock or 8 - Beat

Words and Music by Edward Holland,
Lamont Dozier and Brian Holland

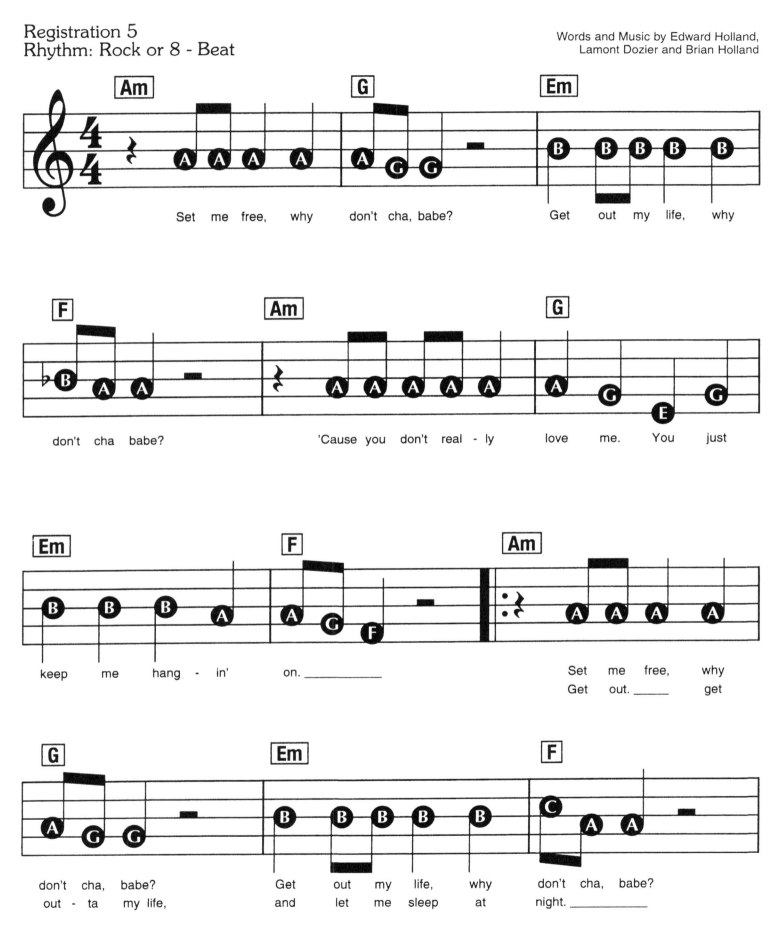

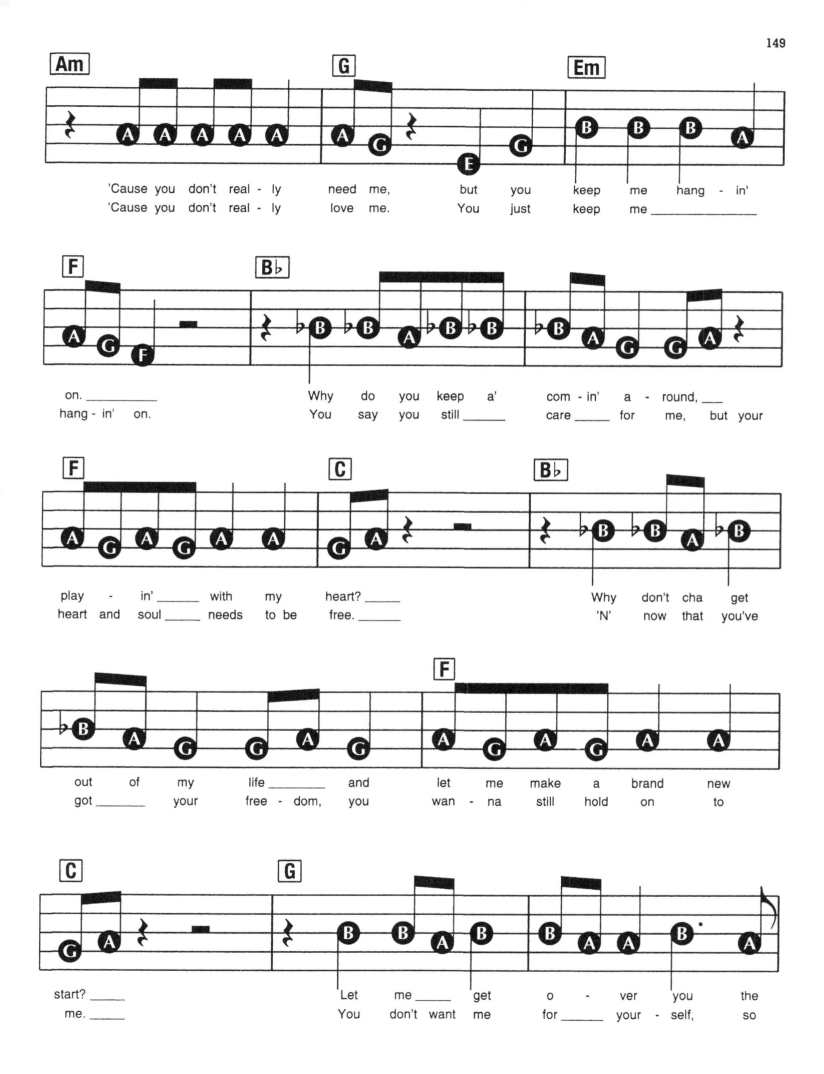

150

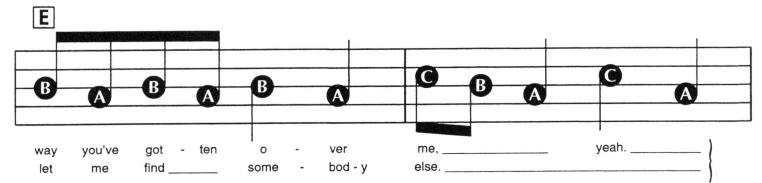

way you've got - ten o - ver me, _____ yeah. _____
let me find _____ some - bod - y else. _____

Set me free, why don't cha, babe? Get out my life, why

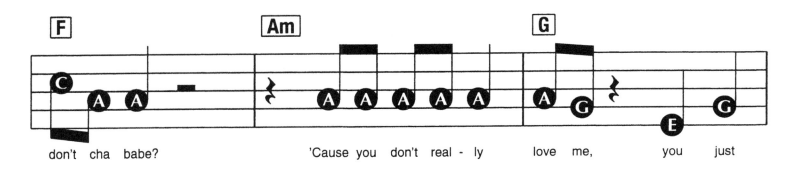

don't cha babe? 'Cause you don't real - ly love me, you just

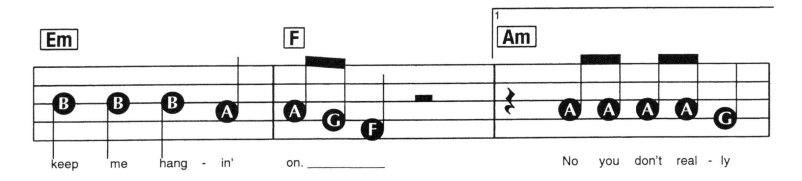

keep me hang - in' on. _____ No you don't real - ly

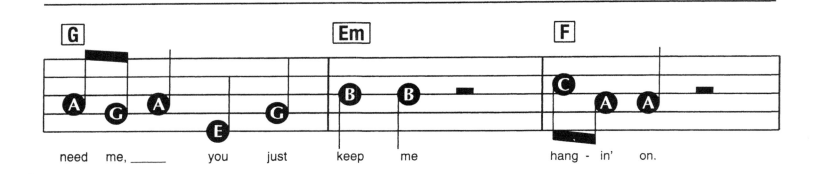

need me, _____ you just keep me hang - in' on.

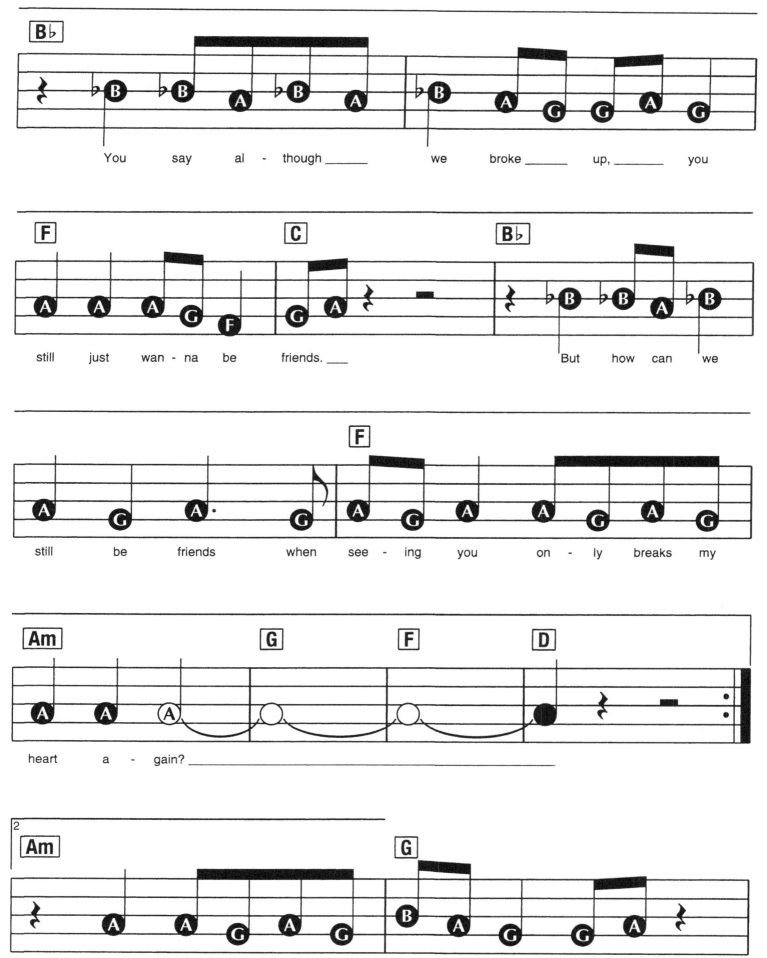

Bb

You say al - though _____ we broke _____ up, _____ you

F   C   Bb

still just wan - na be friends. ___   But how can we

F

still be friends when see - ing you on - ly breaks my

Am   G   F   D

heart a - gain? _____

2
Am   G

Why don't cha be a man _____ a - bout it,